ACCOLADES FOR THE PROFIT BLEED

Vicki Suiter's THE PROFIT BLEED *is a super-powerful playbook full of practical techniques and systems for strengthening your business and creating profit!*

—Steve Chandler, author of
THE SMALL BUSINESS MILLIONAIRE

In her book, Vicki has managed to deliver her considerable knowledge and expertise in the workings of the construction industry in a format that is understandable, and intuitive. The narrative is skillfully crafted to make the information more accessible by humanizing her approach, utilizing her own story and the story of others. Vicki's fresh approach to this topic makes it timeless and an essential read for people who strive to improve their lives, businesses, and their bottom line.

—Steve Rempe, President and
CEO, Rempe Construction, Inc.

Why is it that contractors can build almost any structure with their eyes closed, yet struggle with building consistent profits? The answer is in having the right tools. And that is exactly what Vicki Suiter's book is —the ideal tool to build your profitable business.

—Mike Michalowicz,
author of PROFIT FIRST

In her book, Vicki takes the complexity of business, and distills it into easy to read and understand elements. The book makes generating more profits, time and fun from your business completely accessible. The clear strategies Vicki provides at the end of each chapter gives you the tools you need to implement those strategies right on the spot.

—Michael Port, NY Times, WSJ bestselling author of Steal the Show and Book Yourself Solid

Numbers are tools and like most 'unknowns' can be frightening without having some understanding first. The Profit Bleed by Vicki Suiter provides the understanding that business owners need to grow a sustainable business that is successful and fun. I plan to refer clients to this book so they can start enjoying their journeys to create the profits they desire.

—May McCarthy, President, Bizzultz, LLC, and author of The Path to Wealth

Knowledge is the quickest and safest path to success in any area of life. Vicki Suiter has encapsulated the strategies used by contracting companies who are highly successful. Success can be learned, and this book is a highly effective way to learn it.

—Verne Harnish, Founder, Entrepreneurs' Organization (EO) and author of Scaling Up (Rockefeller Habits 2.0)

Knowledge is power. If you're a contracting company, you want what's in this book. Now. Vicki Suiter delivers the knowledge - and the practical strategies - used by companies succeeding at the very highest levels, so that you can learn and apply their secrets to enjoy the prosperity you deserve. Stop the bleed. This is your quickest and safest pathway to success.

—Walt Hampton, J.D., President and COO, Book Yourself Solid® Worldwide

Not only does Vicki have a deep understanding of how to build a profitable and successful contracting business, she also understands the psychology of human beings, and how to help us be better sales people, managers and leaders. A must read for anyone looking to grow their contracting company.

—Marisa Murgatroyd, Founder
and CEO, Live Your Message

This book provides compelling insights and strategies for identifying the root causes of business growth stagnation and waning profit margins. It's a must read for managers and business owners looking to take their businesses and careers to the next level.

—John Hanley, Founder and CEO,
Quantum Transformation Academy
and author of GETTING FROM WHERE
YOU ARE TO WHERE YOU WANT TO BE

This parable tracks the progress of two remodelers, partners, as they begin to make the changes they know are essential... if they're to stay in business. Vicki addresses an array of common issues that hold remodelers back – providing easy-to-understand guidance on how to improve results in each of these important areas. Pulse Points summarize the advice, giving the reader a list of actions to be completed. Her advice is delivered in a down-to-earth manner, backed by detail on how taking certain actions will change the trajectory of the business. Remodelers who read this book will recognize themselves on every page and will be able to apply this sound advice to their own companies, watching the promised improvements develop at each step of the journey.

—Victoria Downing, President and
Chief Inspiration Officer,
Remodelers Advantage, Inc.

VICKI SUITER

THE PROFIT BLEED

**HOW MANAGING MARGIN CAN SAVE YOUR
CONTRACTING BUSINESS**

Copyright © 2018 Vicki Suiter

All Rights Reserved

No part of this book may be reproduced or transmitted in any form or by any means, electronic or mechanical, including photocopying, recording, or by any information storage and retrieve system, without permission in writing from the publisher.

Disclaimer

This publication is designed to provide information about the subject matter covered. It is sold with the understanding that neither the author nor the publisher is engaged by the reader to render legal, financial, investment, accounting or other professional service or advice. The purpose of this book is to educate and entertain. Neither the author nor the publisher, Summit Press Publishing, shall have any liability or responsibility to any person or entity with respect to any loss or damage caused, or alleged to be caused, directly or indirectly by the information contained in this book.

ISBN: 978-1983932670

Library of Congress Control Number: 2018936740

For more information, visit
https://suiterbusinessbuilders.com

Published by

Summit Press Publishing
Green Cove Springs, Fl
phone 860-306-4057
fax 860-281-2750
https://summit-success.com

Cover design by Junnifer Baya; interior design by S. Peter Lewis

To my mom,

thank you for always believing in me.

ACKNOWLEDGMENTS

To my clients, who have taught me so much. Your courage and dedication has been inspiring. Thank you for trusting me, and for allowing me into your businesses and your lives.

To Ann Sheybani, my writing coach, for your eloquent way of helping me find my words and speak from my authentic voice. For teaching me how to be a better writer and for your encouragement every step of the way – thank you. Without you, this book would still be a hopeful thought.

To the team of professionals who brought their best to the editing and refining of the words on these pages – thank you.

To my long-time client and friend Steve Rempe – thank you for reading the first draft, giving me your honest feedback, and for the encouragement every step of the way. It gave me the courage to know that what I had to say was worth sharing.

To my kids Kari, Taylor and Kelsey – the amazing people you are – thank you for all the love, support and encouragement throughout the writing of this book, and every day. I feel truly blessed to be your mom.

To my always supportive, loving, encouraging, and insightful husband Tim, thank you for being my partner in life, growth and transformation. Thank you for always believing in me and seeing the best in me – you make my world better every day.

CONTENTS

■ ■ ■

INTRODUCTION
1

CHAPTER 1 – PRICING
13

CHAPTER 2 – SALES
39

CHAPTER 3 – PRODUCTION
63

CHAPTER 4 – FEEDBACK
81

CHAPTER 5 – PROJECT MANAGEMENT
103

CHAPTER 6 – TAKE AN EAGLE'S VIEW OF YOUR BUSINESS
119

INTRODUCTION

At first glance their growth looked amazing—they'd gone from $3 million a year in annual revenues to $15 million in just three years. And that was in a down economy. But scanning further down the page to the bottom line, I spotted trouble. Serious trouble. Constantine Contracting (not their real name) had gone from $500,000 in net profit to a loss of $250,000 in that same period—a staggering loss—especially given the huge climb in revenues. As I read the numbers out loud, the looks on the partners' faces revealed the deep sense of disappointment and frustration that had prompted them to reach out to me in the first place.

When Constantine's CEO, Bruce, first called me, he explained that they were struggling with not making enough profits. They had constant cash flow challenges, and a huge amount of tension between him and his partner, Scott. Each of them managed a different area of the business—Bruce was marketing, estimating, and sales; Scott was production, finance, and human resources. The two heads blamed each other for problems outside of their control.

Bruce and Scott had been working long days and weekends in an attempt to keep their business alive. Losing money at a rapid rate, cash flow being tight all the time, and being perpetually exhausted left them feeling like it was all coming to a head. They were doing everything they knew to do to keep their business alive, and it wasn't working.

Unfortunately, I'd seen scenarios like this before.

Over the past twenty-five years, I've gained a reputation in the contracting industry as the person who can help you create more profits, time, and fun in your business; I'm the person who can help you get your business healthy again, and thriving.

Now listen: I don't have a magic wand that I wave and "poof" your business is saved. What I do have, however, is knowledge. I know that business doesn't have to be complicated. When you understand the most critical elements that drive the success of your company, then you'll have more control over its destiny. Knowing the handful of key numbers to manage is a big part of that. While they're never the whole story, numbers almost always serve as the foundation of the work I do.

See, numbers light up what's really happening in a company. They illuminate a pattern of behavior and often, as I dig deeper in conversation with a client, they reveal beliefs that drive those behaviors. Numbers illuminate a picture of where a company has been, the choices the owners have made, and where a company's core issues really exist. This may sound too complicated, but it's not; utilizing these numbers is something you can learn to do in your own business, and in this book, I'm going to show you how.

What I love about numbers is that they inform us; they give us clarity. That clarity gives us the confidence to take actions that allow us to regain control of our businesses. Numbers give us the ability to clearly understand the actions we need to take to move closer to reaching our goals, and fulfilling our dreams. There's no judgment in numbers. They're not personal. Numbers just are.

Now I should say that a number in and of itself doesn't mean much; but that number in relation to something else, brings a whole other level of meaning and depth. You might think of it this way: numbers are like the heartbeat that keeps your business alive. Take care of them, and you'll see their strength reflected in the health and success of your business. Neglect them, and you'll eventually find your business on life support.

While the numbers vary from company to company, and the stories change, most clients who walk into my office each week have similar troubles. Working hard, not making the profits they'd like, and not clear about how to go about changing all that. For obvious reasons, it's usually not much fun for anyone involved anymore. Working hard and not getting ahead is frustrating and demoralizing.

It always tugs at my heart when I see this. I want people to win; I want them to succeed; I want them to have lives that are fulfilling, work that is rewarding, and businesses that thrive. I want them to be able to fulfill that dream they had once upon a time when they had the courage to hang out their shingle and forge the path to business ownership.

This desire is one of the reasons I was compelled to go back to college and complete my degree at the age of thirty-five. I wanted to learn how to help other business owners because I understood the struggle.

I get it on a very personal level. It takes enormous courage and fortitude to be a business owner. It takes a willingness to risk, to put yourself out there, with no guarantee people will want what you have to offer. It also takes faith to swim in highly competitive waters. All this knowing that eight out of ten new businesses fail in the first five years.

I lived through these challenges. And when I learned how to help myself, the lessons translated.

When I graduated in 1997, I discovered a few amazing things. First, I wasn't the only one who could do what I did for clients; there was plenty of competition. Second, even with said competition, I didn't need to work fifty to sixty hours a week to make enough money to pay the mortgage. Third, if I worked smarter rather than harder, I could build sustained success.

In the two years I'd been in school, I worked an average of thirty-five hours a week, versus the fifty to sixty I was working before. I also made more money in my consulting business each of those years than I had in any of the years prior, all while attending class at night and on weekends. That entire experience taught me to think outside the box, to see new possibilities, to figure out how to go about replicating myself even when I didn't think it was possible. I also learned that when you have clarity, you are more confident; when you have more confidence, you take more powerful actions—this, more than anything else, has allowed me to help my clients grow their companies and create sustained success over these past thirty years.

While business can often feel complex, developing that foundational clarity can be quite simple: provided you understand a few numbers; provided you understand the key elements that drive the success of your business, and learn to manage them—both in terms of the numbers themselves and how you and your team takes ownership of them.

Think of it this way: When you show up at the doctor's office, he takes your vitals, and compares them against certain benchmarks that are "within the range of normal." If your temperature or heart rate is too high, he'll dig a little deeper. If other key symptoms are "out of the normal range," he may order blood work, an x-ray, or more tests. In a similar way, your business has certain "vital signs" you'll want to track to allow you to keep your finger on the pulse of its health. Businesses that are losing money may well be in danger of dying. To ignore the vitals, the key numbers that tell the story, can be downright suicidal.

The partners at Constantine Contracting just kept pushing ahead every day not looking at the vital signs of their business. They didn't look at financial reports each month; weren't tracking job performance; didn't have a gross profit margin goal when bidding; didn't have a sales close rate benchmark. Not having any benchmarks meant they were ignoring their vitals, and hoping for the best. They were not leading and directing where they wanted their business to go—they were responding and reacting, hoping it ended up somewhere good.

It's amazing how long human beings will endure pain. We get used to it, and adapt to the discomfort. We do this with our bodies; ignore the assortment of aches, particularly when we get older. We assume there's nothing to be done about it, or that it will eventually resolve. Similarly, business owners and leaders figure out workarounds for problems—work more hours, do more and more—hoping things will change. They do that until one day the pain becomes so unbearable; until they cannot take it any longer; until they are on the brink of disaster. That's when they pick up the phone and ask for help. Or just give up.

My basic presupposition is that people are always doing the best they can, so when they call me, I don't judge. I completely understand that change is hard for us humans, and I also know that until there's enough pain or discomfort, we don't take different actions.

Beyond the perceived work involved, it's human nature to avoid looking at numbers you suspect do *not* look good. It's why we avoid standing on the scale after a two-week cruise, or looking at our credit card statement and examining the interest paid. But the truth is, knowing your numbers will allow you to know where you stand. In doing so, you'll know the gap that exists between where you are now, and where you want to be. That's where your real power lies.

When you know your numbers—the essential numbers that drive your profitability—then you can start to make choices with your eyes wide open. You can start to have more control over your bottom line, and begin to drive profits with more clarity and confidence. The clarity you'll gain out of knowing your numbers is critical to your success. That clarity will give you more confidence in bidding and selling work. That confidence will enable you to take more powerful actions and draw more people to your business.

If you're thinking to yourself, *I'm not a numbers person,* or *I'm not an accountant, that's why I've got a bookkeeper / CPA / Accounting staff,* please understand: I'm not talking about accounting or being a numbers fanatic. I'm talking about knowing a handful of simple numbers to track in your business that will give you control over your bottom line, and ultimately, your life. They are the numbers that will let you keep a "pulse" on the health of your company.

Trust me, I know what it feels like to work endless hours trying to grow a business, wondering when you'll hit your limit, wrestling with challenges and roadblocks that feel insurmountable. Constantine Contracting was at that breaking point, and ready to make a change—ready to look for the source of the breakdown, to confront their vitals.

I expect you're ready to make a change, too.

I worked with Constantine for months, meeting regularly to guide and support them through the process. Now I'd like to take you through the process, too.

As with Constantine, we'll start with the numbers and address other key elements from that rock-solid foundation/crystal-clear vantage point. I'll show you the key drivers for where profits are made and lost. You'll do an inventory of your own business and begin to develop a plan for increasing your profits. You'll get tools and resources that will help you calculate your overhead breakeven percentage, find out how to predict revenues well in advance of that cold, hard moment it shows up on your profit and loss statement. You'll gain clarity on what key numbers and results to track that will help you "keep your finger on the pulse" of your business.

I've included a number of resources in this book to help you tailor this information to your own company. At the end of each chapter is a list of "pulse point" items you'll want to track that relate to that particular part of your business. In the appendix, I've included links, resources, and checklists (referenced throughout the book) that will help you put what you're learning here into action.

If you follow the system and strategies I've laid out for you in this book, you'll regain control—of your business, your time, your life. You'll start to enjoy yourself again and make the profits you desire. You'll experience a new level of sustainable success.

Let's get started.

If you want to make a consistent profit...

you need to know your real costs, and build the right markups for overhead and profit into your pricing.

CHAPTER 1

PRICING

Bruce and Scott sat with me in my office, ready to look for the source of the breakdown, ready to confront their vitals.

The partners couldn't understand where they'd gone wrong. Constantine Contracting had grown in revenues by leaps and bounds, but their profits were waning. In their largest year of revenue, they'd lost more money than they'd made in the prior four years combined. They'd been playing the volume game. They were running blind, hoping the "grow sales" strategy would give them an advantage in the marketplace. With enough volume, they figured, they'd grow their bottom line. Nothing could have been further from the truth. Their lack of clarity was killing their business. Their bottom line was under water. And they were tired. It's exhausting having to chase after work just to stay alive. It's the thing that keeps you up at night, which keeps you from having a life.

I studied the numbers while Bruce and Scott wrung their hands over cold cups of coffee. It didn't take long to see that what they were missing was a clear understanding of their real costs, and that they had no profit margin goals. None. They had priced themselves nearly out of business. Without these things—an understanding of real costs and profit margin goals—you end up with a sick gross profit margin, which is what Constantine had.

All issues lead to gross profit margin. If you don't manage it closely, it can take the knees out from under you; it can destroy your company. As a matter of fact, more often than not, large fluctuations or drops in gross profit margin, is the key reason many contracting businesses are not making the profits they'd like. Focusing on the gross profit margin is kind of like taking the pulse—it's the first thing you check in when sizing up health issues.

To start: there's a misconception among many in the contracting industry that you can only mark up projects at "what the market will bear." In response, they use numbers they hear from architects, other contractors, designers, or trades people.

The real problem is that these nervous contractors have zero idea of what their real overhead percentage looks like. They don't know what it actually costs to run their business. When they don't know the actual costs of running their business and base their markup on what they see in the industry rather than their own needs, they're throwing themselves under the proverbial bus time and time again. They're setting themselves up for failure.

■ ■ ■

Now, I'm not saying you should ignore industry numbers entirely; that can be its own deathblow. At the same time, you need to take them with a grain of salt and realize those numbers don't necessarily tell the whole story.

Constantine Contracting had intentionally lowered their prices in order to get more work in a down economy. While the strategy worked to increase revenues, they actually had no idea what it really cost to run their business. So every time they bid work, they were putting markup figures in the bids that would have them losing money every time. This was decimating their gross profit margin; this is why they were hemorrhaging.

Now was the time to explore Constantine's pricing practices, how they went about choosing their figures, what factors they took into the accounting of them, or left out altogether.

I explained to the partners that in thirty years there had been less than a handful of times I'd told a contracting client they should consider lowering their prices.

"There's no way we can increase our prices," Bruce said. "You don't understand… our competitors will get the project."

To which I replied, "It's not the sales price that's the problem. It's your lack of awareness of the true costs involved in your calculation, as well as your lack of faith in the numbers."

When you don't know your numbers, you become vague and hedge your bets; you leave a lot of wiggle room; and people sense that, so they don't trust you. They figure you're just another lying, cheating contractor; then it's not the sales price that's the problem, it's you. When you know your numbers cold, on the other hand, what it's going to take to do the work, you're going to have more confidence in the sales process, and that confidence will allow you to educate your client. Then you'll smell trustworthy; you'll earn the business.

The partners looked at each other, mouth agape. Bruce looked guilty.

Without a clear understanding of their numbers, the thought of arbitrarily increasing prices terrified them. And understandably so. You shouldn't increase prices arbitrarily; you should only do so when you know the real cost of doing the work. Once you know your real costs, then you're grounded in the facts. It's from that place of being grounded that you can look at your bid and assess what you need to do if the price is out of the client's budget. But first, you need to tell the truth about your real costs. As the saying goes, *the truth shall set you free.*

I understand that numbers intimidate a lot of people. They think digging into the numbers is synonymous with doing accounting or math. I'm going to beat the drum here, just for a minute. Knowing your numbers is not about performing accounting tricks or math feats. It's about being clear on the basic costs of doing the work and running your business. When you're clear about that, everything gets easier. You lay a good foundation; your building stands up. Now I'll put down the drumstick.

The goal of understanding your numbers is twofold. Number one, it's to know how to price things properly so you don't go out of business. Number two, it's to develop the confidence so that when you go in with a quote, there's nothing shady about how you're operating—which helps you give off a vibe that's far more appealing to people than that disingenuous low ball offer.

Knowing what it takes to do the work, the costs of producing that work, the costs of running your business, and the minimum you need to mark up to meet your profit goals, that's when you'll have more confidence in the whole sales process, and exude trustworthiness. That trust will allow you to educate your client about options and choices they can make to lower their costs, thereby the bid price. The entire process of deeply vetting your numbers will also allow you to know *what is and is not* included in the scope of work, and you'll be able to clearly communicate that to the client. And that's attractive.

So let's talk about how to trust your numbers and create estimates that will sustain and build your profitable business.

We could write an entire book on how to create an estimate. There are as many ways to get it done as there are contractors; and everyone has their own methodology. As a matter of fact, people are so fond of their own particular method, I've learned not to argue with them about the "best approach." But no matter how you go about the details of estimating, you need to incorporate some fundamental steps into your process. You've got to know your cost for producing the work (or COGS, cost of goods sold), mark up to cover overhead and make a profit, and manage your gross profit margins.

KNOW YOUR COST FOR PRODUCING THE WORK

Before anything else, you need to be clear about your *real* cost of doing the work.

Even with the knowledge that it costs you a certain amount to do the work—you've got lumber to purchase, say, or people to hire—many contractors resist digging deep into their real costs. It's a lot of work to re-figure unit prices (if that's the current approach to bidding). It takes a lot of time to job cost work as it's being performed, and then look back at historical data to inform you about how to bid scope in future work. And frankly, it can be confusing to know all the real costs of having that employee.

Some costs are hard to ignore because they're right out in plain sight—materials, equipment rentals, or subcontractors, for example. Other costs, the sort that get approximated, require some sleuthing.

The most difficult one to nail down is labor. It's your biggest uncertain variable given the different degrees of skills and experience of your staff, as well as the scope of work and the accuracy with which it's been defined and communicated ahead of time. Using historical job cost information along with a set of plans and clear scope will help you identify those hours.

In the absence of a clear set of plans/scope, many successful contractors will communicate in the documentation and when presenting to the client what assumptions they're using when bidding and what is and is not included.

And while contractors are afraid of bidding wars, of losing business to the competitive company with the sharper pencil, the very act of clarifying your real costs is what gives you the confidence to negotiate contracts and increase your close rate, because you're not secretly worried about losing your shirt. When you're clear about your numbers, your prospective client will respond to your certainty. They won't look at you with suspicion, wondering how you're going to sock it to them to recoup your losses.

> We'll talk about how to build trust with prospects and become the contractor of choice in the next chapter.

Understanding your COGS is an essential first step, and this is where I wanted to go with Constantine. "Let's get clear about your true cost of doing the work and set a gross profit margin goal that will support your growth and make you profitable," I said to the partners. "Because it's clear to me that you're not charging your customers enough."

> Cost of Goods Sold (COGS), also referred to as Direct Costs, are the costs directly related to producing the services you offer as a contracting company. You want to include them in your bids. Here's a rule of thumb: if you weren't doing that work, what costs would you not incur? Those are the costs you want to include: things like materials, labor, liability insurance, subcontractors, and equipment.

I pointed at several columns of digits on the computer screen. The partners shifted in their seats, coughed. At first blush, this looked like a lot of numbers to the Constantine partners, I was sure. When you first look, you too might feel a little confused or overwhelmed when looking at *your* numbers. But stick with me for a moment or two because once you've got the overview, you'll understand where I'm going with this. "These numbers here," I pointed out, "these are what are getting you into trouble. These are your employees' true burden costs."

KNOW YOUR FULLY-BURDENED LABOR COST

A fully burdened labor cost includes gross wage, employer taxes, workers' compensation insurance, local taxes, as well as benefits (medical, dental, life, 401K, profit sharing, vacation), and other related costs such as cell phones and auto reimbursement.

To begin, ask yourself this question: *What costs would I not incur if I did not have this person working for me?* We're talking expenses associated with having them *just* show up—not including overhead expenses or profit.

See appendix for a resource that will help you calculate your *total* cost of an employee.

KNOW HOW MANY HOURS IT WILL TAKE

Having a clear understanding of how many hours it will take to do each phase of the project is another critical piece of determining an accurate COGS number.

MARK UP TO COVER OVERHEAD AND MAKE A PROFIT

Once the COGS is clearly identified, the next step to insuring a project will make money is adding on a markup for overhead and profit. This is the piece that will allow you to run a successful and profitable contracting business.

The simple definition of overhead markup is the percentage you add into your calculations—into your bid—to cover the cost of running your business. This percentage is what you need just to break even.

It's a very misunderstood number. People often mistakenly take the percentage off their profit and loss or income statement as their overhead mark-up percentage. This is not the correct number; if you use this number, you'll bleed money, as that percentage is lower than your actual overhead breakeven percentage.

For example, you may hear numbers like ten percent overhead and five percent profit thrown around; yet much of the time, the people who spout these figures have no idea what their real overhead costs are; nor do they have a goal for the profit they want to make.

It's natural to go along with the industry belief "this is all the market will bear, so it doesn't really matter what my real overhead costs are, or what I want to make in profit. I have to just charge what the market will bear and hope I can cut the costs when I'm doing the work, or make it up in volume." Operating by this mindset is a losing game. Truth be told, you're never able to "make up profit" in the field. And trying to make it up in volume will only exhaust you. Looking at the partners while we talked, it was clear to me that they hadn't been to a gym in years, nor did they sleep more than five hours a night. No wonder they chain-drank coffee.

While the overhead percentage will vary depending on the size of your company, the truth of the matter is that the actual overhead percentage for most contractors is much higher than ten percent. This means that when charging $100,000 for a project, instead of "giving away" $10,000 to the cost of completing that project, they're "giving away" $15,000 or $20,000, if they're lucky. That additional five or ten percent overhead comes right off the bottom line, which is usually way too slim to begin with. As for marking up five percent for profit—you're making a mistake in thinking you're making five percent on the bottom line—your return will in fact be around four percent. On $500,000 in revenue, that's a loss of $5,000 right to the bottom line.

I showed the partners how to correctly calculate the markup percentage they needed. They leaned over the desk as I opened their most recent profit and loss statement on my laptop. They had made the same mistake I just described. When they saw the difference in values, they were horrified. The number they'd been using to mark up direct costs to cover overhead was sixteen percent; they should have been using nineteen percent. With direct costs of $10 million the prior year, they'd just lost out on $310,000 in profits. The loss from the prior year was starting to make more sense to them.

Before you can calculate a markup, you've got to know your overhead breakeven percentage—that number where you won't make a profit, but you won't lose money either. Breaking even may be bad (after all, we're in the business to turn a profit), but losing money is much worse. So before you can calculate a markup, you've got to know your overhead breakeven percentage—that number where you won't make a profit, but you won't lose money either.

> To calculate your overhead breakeven percentage: Take a sample of data from your profit and loss statement that spans one year and divide by direct costs/COGS. This is the amount you must mark up COGS just to break even. For more detailed information on how to calculate your overhead breakeven percentage, visit my website and download my free article titled "Calculating Overhead Breakeven Percentage." https://theprofitbleed.com/resources

THERE ARE ONLY TWO WAYS TO INCREASE PROFITABILITY

The partners looked at the overhead markup percentage I had calculated. "We'd never be able to tack that percentage on and make it fly," Bruce said. They looked at me as if they could dismiss reality, and carry on as they'd been doing. As if their numbers were lying.

You might share their reluctance.

But let's be clear here—there are only two ways to affect your bottom line: increase revenue or decrease costs. And there are only two ways to do either of those things: bring in more money or stop overspending.

To increase revenue, you can add more services, thereby selling more, or increase your markups. To decrease spending, you can lower the costs of running your business, or become more efficient in production, thus lowering production costs.

Constantine had focused on selling more, and that hadn't worked. It had also left them exhausted, disheartened, and broke. Scott was on the brink of divorce.

Now, I get how trying harder, working longer hours, and taking on more projects might seem like the solution, but sometimes more isn't the answer. Sometimes taking on more, without limits, is the problem. The more sustainable option to bringing in more revenue is to increase your markups. If you think the market won't bear you marking up "that much" consider this: if the customer doesn't cover those costs, they're coming out of your pocket. There is no other source.

"Well, if we think these numbers won't fly with our customers, what else can we do?" Bruce asked.

I pointed at the top number in the equation, at overhead costs. "Are they too high for a company doing the volume you're doing?"

One look and the answer was simple. You see, that's the nice thing about math: it's brutally simple. Straightforward and unemotional, numbers will tell you your options. It's entirely up to you which to choose.

Increase revenue and your COGS will go up. If you can grow revenues without increasing your overhead costs much, that's great—the result is your overhead breakeven percentage will then go down; you won't have to mark up as much just to break even. You can mark up less, if you choose, or mark up the same amount with more going to profit. This is simply numerator and denominator stuff.

Unfortunately, when companies grow too quickly, as Constantine had, breakdowns start to occur, and people have a tendency to throw money at the problems in an attempt to fix the hemorrhaging. And throwing money at problems rarely ever fixes the source of the problem.

Constantine Contracting's overhead had grown, the partners agreed, and they weren't doing a good job at controlling their spending. They started hiring people furiously when the volume went up thinking that would fix the breakdowns that were happening at breakneck speed.

"Do you have an operating budget for the company?" I asked, "So you know where you're overspending?" They shook their heads no.

I made some notes for myself to return to this topic a bit down the road. Constantine would need an operating budget to make a plan for bringing down their overhead costs, which would help. But we still needed to return to markups—this time to discuss marking up for profits.

> One way to plan for more profits and controlling overhead costs is to have an operating budget for your company.

Before we get deeper into marking up for profit, let me define net profit and net profit margin. That way we'll all be on the same page.

Net profit is what's left over after you pay yourself your salary and cover all operating costs. (Your salary, by the way, should be included in your overhead calculations.) It's meant for re-investing back into the business, or putting money in reserves for a rainy day, or when you have a few too many slow paying clients, or for making that asset purchase. It's for building financial strength in your company. When you have financial strength, you're building a more solid foundation on which to grow. You feel more secure, less desperate about cash flow (remember, desperation smells bad).

So how do you build greater financial strength so you feel and appear composed? You have a clear net profit margin goal for your business.

Net profit margin is the percentage rate of return you want to generate *after* your salary. Based on my experience in working with hundreds of contracting companies, I knew that ten percent was a good target to shoot for. The same will likely be true for your business unless you do a very large amount of volume (over $30 million).

When you're clear on what net profit you want to make, it becomes easier to bid with profit in mind. When you know how much you should mark up to cover your overhead, and know how much you need to mark up to make a profit, you'll have more confidence in bidding and negotiating work. One number leads to the next in a logical fashion. When it can be no other way, there's no hemming or hawing.

Here's a little math trickery: If you want to make a ten percent net profit for your company, you'll have to have an overall markup of a little over eleven percent. When I say "overall markup" I mean once you've marked up for overhead, and then for profit. This is the first step to reaching your net profit goals.

The concept was getting clearer for the Constantine partners. They began nodding their heads. For the first time I could see they were no longer fighting what I was saying. It was as though the lights had gone on, and the whole concept of either mark up more, or cut your costs had sunk in. They were ready to tackle the next piece.

How to mark up to reach desired profits

Using Constantine's financial data we calculated their overhead breakeven percentage: almost nineteen percent; and they agreed they wanted a target of ten percent net profit. Armed with this information, I was able to show them the simple math for marking up the cost of doing the work to reach their goal:

Cost of Goods Sold (COGS):	$50,000
Overhead markup:	x 18.7%
Breakeven amount:	$59,350
Profit markup:	x 11.11%
Contract / Bid amount:	$65,945
Gross profit (contract/bid less COGS)	$15,945
Gross profit margin (profit / contract)	24.17%

To take the point a little further, I showed them how, after applying the overhead cost to this job, they would yield a ten percent net profit:

Gross profit (contract/bid less COGS)	$15,945
Overhead (18.7% of COGS)	-$9,350
Net profit (gross profit – overhead)	$6,595
Net profit margin (gross profit – overhead)	10.00%

"OK," Bruce said. "I get that we have to mark up more, but that's not a straightforward process in bidding. Our markups will vary. They'll depend on how we do a job, if the work is self-performed, or if we've got subcontractors, materials, or equipment rental. Labor is where our highest markup is. So how do we reconcile it all?"

MANAGING GROSS PROFIT MARGIN

It's very common for contractors to mark up materials, subcontractors, and labor at different rates, and you should.

The best way to make sure you've got the right overall markup on projects is to manage the gross profit margin—or your rate of return. Because of the varying nature of markups in bidding, this is the one way to insure you are pricing to make a profit.

I explained how to calculate gross profit margin on a project once the bid was complete to insure your project will meet your company gross profit margin goals. Here is the formula:

Bid price	$65,945
Less estimated costs for doing the work (COGS)	($50,000)
Gross profit is the difference between these two	$15,945
Gross profit margin is calculated by taking that gross profit dollars and dividing it by the bid price. This is your rate of return.	24.17%

Now that they knew the formula, I suggested they verify gross profit margin on every bid before it goes out the door. Because the gross profit margin for the year is composed of the gross profit margin for every project done during that year, one begets the other.

"If gross profit margin for each project is not high enough, look where you may need to adjust the markup on certain line items, or where you could add line items that would cover your overhead costs."

The partners seemed to think they could do that.

> Always check bid prices before an estimate is sent to the customer. The formula is simple:
> *Total contract / bid price - cost of goods sold =* gross profit
> *Gross profit ÷ total contract / bid price =* gross profit margin

If you consistently manage bids (and your company) to meet a target gross profit margin, you're going to dramatically increase your odds of making a consistent profit. If you make a consistent profit, you've got yourself a business with a healthy, beating heart.

> To set a gross profit margin goal for your company, visit my website to download the free Markup and Margin Chart so you can see how much to mark up overall to reach your desired gross profit margin goal.
> https://theprofitbleed.com/resources

As Bruce, Scott, and I wrapped up that meeting on pricing, we agreed that they'd have to pick a strategy for bidding and charging more. They acknowledged that the very thought of charging more made them downright nervous. The whole topic might be making you a bit nervous, too. That's OK. Nervous is good.

Because the thing that makes people the most nervous also has the power to remake their business. It's knowing the numbers (remember: there is no one strategy out there. Your job is to identify the one that best fits your needs, and then stick to it). When you know your numbers, you stop deluding yourself, and stop driving your business six feet under. And when you develop the confidence with your numbers, you'll be very attractive to clients.

PULSE POINTS

1. Check that the cost assumptions you're using in bidding are accurate. This includes verifying the fully burdened cost of employees as well as the accurate overhead markup percentage.
2. Have a profit goal and mark up estimates enough to reach that desired profit goal.
3. Check gross profit margin on a bid before sharing with prospects to ensure that you've met your gross profit margin goal.

For tools and resources that will let you get your finger on the pulse of your business go to: https://theprofitbleed.com/resources

If you want to make a consistent profit...

you need a sales process. One that allows you to stand out from the competition, be the preferred contractor, and stack the odds in your favor of closing more contracts.

CHAPTER 2

SALES

As the Constantine partners absorbed what I was saying about pricing, and the need to price to make a profit, I could see Bruce fidgeting. As the conversation transitioned to how to effectively close more sales with higher prices, he couldn't contain himself anymore.

"Listen, we were bidding like crazy before we lowered our prices, and weren't closing enough work. Now that you're telling us to raise our prices, I'm concerned I'm going to have to go back to bidding twice as much work just to get the same number of projects."

It wasn't the first time I'd heard that from a business owner. I explained to Bruce that I completely appreciated his concern. "Are you open to hearing a different way to approach sales that may in fact allow you to bid *less* work?" I asked. He nodded, and leaned in.

I told him that a sale occurs in multiple steps; and this is where a lot of people get tripped up. They think giving a price and then simply waiting for the person to let them know if they want to buy from them or not are all that is necessary. In fact, a sale begins when the phone rings that first time, and is not complete until the job is finished. A sale isn't an event; it's a process.

Having a clear game plan for how sales will flow through your company, and having a clearly articulated sales process, will exponentially increase your odds of closing more sales.

The other common misconception is that a sale is all about price. The truth is, while that number has something to do with why people buy (or don't buy) from you, it plays a much smaller role than you might expect. The ability to close a sale has more to do with perceived value and your ability to solve your customer's problem. It has more to do with your ability to help someone feel safe choosing you. It has more to do with people feeling like they can trust you.

WHY PEOPLE BUY

It's useful to understand why people buy, so let me dig into that topic a bit. According to neuroscientific research, human beings don't like change, of any kind. We're hardwired to maintain status quo. People are more motivated by the avoidance of pain than they are by the promise of rewards. So for you to influence the outcome of your sales efforts, it's important to first understand what motivates the person on the other side to buy; and, second, why they would buy from *you*.

Here's why knowing these things are important...

Right now, when a homeowner comes to you and says, "I want to remodel my house," your first inclination is probably to say, "OK, great. What areas do you want to remodel? Do you have a plan? What do you have in mind? What would you like it to look like?" You want to immediately go to the solution because that's your status quo, that's what you've been trained to do. That's how you think.

"What's the problem with that?" you ask.

The problem is, it doesn't take into account how the homeowner thinks. See, you can use neuroscience to your advantage. You're going to take what we know about the motivation behind change, and work with it instead of ignoring it—or worse, fighting it. In doing so, you'll increase your likelihood of winning the bid.

ASKING QUESTIONS THAT BUILD TRUST AND CONFIDENCE

Since our initial motivator to change is avoidance of pain, you'll first want to find out what caused pain to your customer. You'll explore that pain to better tailor the solution, to better understand what your customer will most value.

"What's not working about how your home is now?" you might ask. "What's sparking this desire to remodel your home?"

After listening to your customer's response, dig deeper; repeat what you heard using their words as much as possible, without paraphrasing—this will let them know they've been heard, which will inspire a greater sense of trust in you.

"So, it's too small—in what way is that a problem for you? It's outdated—outdated how? Oh, the appliances are old, and the fridge is on the fritz. I can appreciate that, and while this might seem like an obvious question to you, what has you wanting to do the whole kitchen and not just replace the appliances?"

As you ask these questions, your client begins to create pictures in their head of what's not working, and connect with why it's not workable for them. This issue is no longer a vague dissatisfaction, but a big, fat thorn in their side.

Now, we're problem solvers, most of us in the service industry; we don't want people to suffer too much. But the truth is, it's our job to clarify for others the need for change and the reasons they may want a given situation to be different. You're going to explore the pain to help clarify it for your customers and better tailor the solution and understand what your customers will most value.

Are you getting the idea?

We've done our clients a service if we can provide them greater clarity, thus more confidence in their choice to do something different, spurring them into action more quickly.

Now, you might think the next step would be to go about solving the problem that's been uncovered with your line of questioning. Nope, you're not ready to do that yet.

When I mentioned this to Bruce and Scott, I could tell they were a bit skeptical. "But if I go into a meeting with a prospect not ready to provide some answers and solutions to their problem, they'll immediately think I'm incompetent" Bruce said. Scott nodded his head in agreement. I explained I was not suggesting they *not* provide solutions, simply that they do a few other things before they get to that stage. Their job is to slow it down, to gather the right information so they could offer a solution that clearly meets their customer's needs. Jumping the gun is what gets everyone into trouble.

The next critical step, I explained, is to find out what they'd like instead. Again, you're going to ask very specific questions. You want them to have a clear picture in their heads of what it will look like, how it will *feel* to be in that new space. You'll ask questions like, "So, your current kitchen is outdated. What will it look like when it's not outdated?"

The customer may answer, "It will have new counter tops, appliances, a new floor that doesn't always get so dirty, and a walk-in pantry, so I don't have to crawl on my knees to the lower cabinets to pull out stuff."

And your response? "So, what will it feel like when you're in your kitchen?"

"Spacious, easy to move around in, and the island in the middle will be the focal point of cooking and gatherings."

"Oh, tell me more about gatherings?"

This is where the customer connects with those feelings we talked about. "I like to entertain. Right now, I don't do it much because I'm so embarrassed by my kitchen."

And this is where you stay with those feelings, not just the painful ones, but also the pleasurable ones any change might create. "So, when you're *not* embarrassed in your kitchen, how will you be feeling? When you make a picture of the kitchen in your head, are there colors you're seeing, or textures, or angles?"

Now you get the prospect to make a picture in her head about what she wants, and you've created a clear "gap" in her brain, a gap between what she has now, and what she wants. The more obvious the gap, the more tension that exists, and the quicker the customer will want to resolve the tension.

Now is the time to offer a solution. Now is when you have a wide-open field to input your ideas, to offer your thoughts on what changes could be made. Now, and not before.

Before I go on, I'd like to talk about the gift of questions. Some people view asking too many questions as being impolite. Others worry that doing so makes them look dumb. Questions, however, are neither of those. They are, instead, a gift. Asking questions of the prospect in a way that helps provide clarity will allow everyone involved to feel confident, and to take more powerful actions. Sometimes people are not clear about what isn't working, or simply bypass the thought because it's uncomfortable, and they just want to focus on what they want. Yet, we all know it was a problem that motivated them to pick up the phone and call you in the first place. When you can reveal that for them (and you), it will provide a much more powerful springboard from which to learn more about what they want—and ultimately, for you to offer the best possible solution.

> The first step in the exploration phase of the sales process is to find out exactly what *isn't* working for the prospect; what has them looking to make a change. Asking questions that allow you to dig deeper and find out as much information as possible will serve both you and the client.
>
> The second step, *before you offer a solution*, is to ask detailed questions about what they would like. *What will it look like when it's as you'd like it to be*? You want them to be making pictures in their head of how it will look and feel.
>
> The third step is to discuss how you can help them to get what they'd like.
>
> Check out my article "The Sales Process" on my website for sample questions with a step-by-step outline.
>
> https://theprofitbleed.com/resources

If you start by following these steps in the exploration phase of the sales process, you'll already start to be perceived as the preferred contractor. Why? You gave the client clarity about what's not working and what it is, in fact, she wants. She is now more confident and ready to act. She feels seen, heard, and understood; you have built trust.

This line of questioning that exposes the gap is one of your greatest tools in the sales process. If you get this concept down, you're going to start to see a dramatic increase in your close rate.

People like to do business with people they trust. They want to feel like the person they chose to remodel their home, work on their business, build their deck, or revamp their garden, understands them and understands their concerns, their needs, their desires. They want to feel that, by being around that person, they can feel good about themselves and the choices they're making. They want to know that you, the service provider, the sales person, understands them. Those are all the factors that go into someone choosing to buy your services.

CUSTOMIZING YOUR SALES PROCESS

So far we've touched on how to ask questions to build trust and confidence. Given that knowing how to ask questions in a powerful way is the cornerstone of a good sales process, I wanted to make those distinctions for Constantine before we moved into creating a customized sales process just for them. It was time to tackle what that would look like.

The partners had been listening quietly to my lesson. Bruce was looking a bit less skeptical, but I could still sense hesitation.

"It feels like a lot of steps, especially with all that questioning. It could take too much time, and time is what I'm short of. What if the customer gets impatient, too?"

"Great questions," I exclaimed. "It is a longer process, and not one you'll find your competition doing. And *that* right there, not your lowball bids that are going to drive your business into the ground, is what will you give you the competitive advantage."

MANAGING EXPECTATIONS

There's a very simple step you can take when the customer first calls, I went on to explain. To avoid stirring impatience, let them know you have a process around bidding that allows you to provide the best possible solution. That process includes asking them some clarifying questions on the phone; and if they decide to proceed, to set up an in-person meeting to discuss another series of questions that will further clarify what they want to change, and what they would ideally like. Explain that from that in-person meeting, you'll do up a proposal and then present that proposal to them in person or via Skype (or whatever video conferencing tool you use). Then ask them if they are OK with that. Wait for an answer. People will say yes ninety-nine percent of the time. At the end of each conversation, remind them of the next step.

"I like that," said Scott. He looked at Bruce. "What do you think of giving it a try?"

"OK," said Bruce, "but it still feels a bit 'salesy' to me."

Clearly there were a few other distinctions I needed to make for Bruce. "A sale is *not* about getting people to buy what they don't want. It's about helping people get what they want. It's about helping them make clear, confident choices. If you let those two things be your focus, it is a game changer."

"Here's the other problem," Bruce said after he'd had a moment to think. "We've been going after volume. We simply don't have the time to take each potential customer through an extensive question-and-answer process. We must move fast, decisively."

I raised one finger. "Volume work has nearly put the nail in your coffin. It's time to put some clear parameters in place so you're not continually chasing your tail, bidding for the sake of bidding. And that starts with a screening process. This will help you determine if someone is worth talking to, working with, or not."

SCREENING FOR THE RIGHT FIT

You'll want the questions you ask in that initial call to include questions that will help you identify if this prospect is a "right fit" for your company. This will eliminate you bidding for tire kickers and those just looking for the lowball price.

Working with Scott and Bruce, we created a matrix that could be used to rate a potential job opportunity. The rating matrix focused primarily on the scope / size of the job.

First, we set a goal for the minimum size job Constantine would take. Then we defined what made for an acceptable location, the required timing for when the work would be done, etc.

If the rating came out below a certain level, Constantine would politely say that they didn't think they were a good fit, and offer to refer another contractor. The homeowner, by the way, is always grateful for the honesty. And Constantine would save precious time by not bidding a job that didn't meet its requirements.

ASKING POWERFUL QUESTIONS

Bruce agreed that once he saw the screening process was working, and he had some traction on the bidding template, he'd take on another step in the sales process; he would begin asking more specific questions when on the phone with a prospect. One step at a time, we agreed, was how this change thing was played. The goal was that once Bruce started doing this consistently, his close rate would go up. He would bid more jobs that were viable, and not waste time on jobs that would likely not pan out or be worth his while.

These additional questions would be designed to let the prospect know that Constantine had a "process" that would take a certain amount of time, and that they would need the customer's buy in. The very fact that the prospect knows Constantine has a process, builds credibility. The prospect can also feel a clear sense of choice. They can take the time to stick with the process, understanding there are multiple steps, particularly if it allows them to clarify the vision, requirements, and scope of their project.

Again, you are building trust and confidence.

It is also your job to make is easy for the prospect to say yes. Easy for them means you're clear in your communication.

> When you show up at the first in-home meeting, have an information packet about your company to leave with them, or email it to them after the first phone call. This will ideally include testimonials.

I turned to Bruce and Scott. "When you begin the process, it will no doubt feel clunky and awkward. That's the way it is for most of my clients. You'll likely find that you'll need to change up the questions to better fit your communication styles. Before long, however, the process will begin to feel natural. You'll become consistent. You'll start getting better information from the customer. The time Bruce spends estimating projects will be less, and his close rates will start to increase."

Bruce and Scott were thinking ahead. They could spot the obstacles, particularly when it came to prospect interactions.

"Let's talk about the follow up," Bruce said. "What's the trick to not sounding needy? Yah, it's great that we'll be asking lots of questions, getting everybody clear. But how do I get someone to call me back after gathering that information? Everyone wants me to just email the bid. I just don't know how to get past that."

"The answer is simple," I said, "get their agreement."

THE POWER OF AGREEMENTS

People naturally want to keep their agreements, so when you have the first call with them, let them know you'll spend ten minutes asking them some questions on the phone, then set up a time to do a walk through. Mention that when the bid is completed, you'll go over the bid with them, either at their home or by phone, and get their buy in. Then ask, "Is that OK with you?" You'll want a clear "yes." Before you hang up the phone, reiterate the next steps, and set up a time when you'll do the walk through.

I should mention here, I've encouraged subcontractor clients of mine to drop the bid off *and* email it. When they got past their initial reluctance and started doing it consistently (with a nice box of chocolates in hand), they found their customers, the GCs, placed them more "top of mind." These GCs began to ask them to bid more work, and they started winning more jobs. All because of those multiple points of contact making it easier to work together. In other words, there's nothing awkward or needy about having an effective follow up process for bidding.

Understand, each part of the sales process is a standalone event: you never sell a project on the first phone call, unless you're doing service work.

■ ■ ■

The first call is simply intended to get an invitation to bid; the in-person meeting is intended to get clarity, build rapport, and trust with the prospect; and the bid presentation meeting is an opportunity to make sure you've provided a solution to the customer's needs, and to close the sale.

Remember, your goal is to provide value, make it easy for the customer to buy from you, to get their buy in.

And once you get the customer's buy in, their agreement, you need to keep up your end of the deal.

Keeping your word, doing what you say you'll do, when you say you'll do it, is the foundation of your reputation. You want to be known as someone who can be trusted. In an industry riddled with dishonesty and subterfuge, I will tell you, if you do nothing else I've shared with you here other than this one thing, you'll increase your close rate, and you'll have people clamoring at your door to work with you. You'll get tons of referrals from happy clients; and you'll stand heads above the competition.

> Other ways to stand out from the competition?
> - Be willing to take responsibility for your mistakes.
> - Be willing to say you don't know, but you'll find out when asked a question to which you really don't know the answer.
> - Be honest with yourself when a project scope is out of your depth, and be willing to pass because the risk associated with those projects can take your business down.

Clarity breeds happiness for everyone involved. We're talking about clarity here: how can you create greater clarity for yourself and for your customer? When you're clear—whether clarity takes the form of knowing the customer's pain, challenges, needs and desires, or knowing clear scope, and budget—it's easier to take control of the process because you'll know what you're actually doing. And so will they.

BID TRACKING

Now that you know the kind of jobs you want to take on, the type of customers you want to sell to, you'll need to track what's coming in the door. Having the right data will allow you to better manage the estimating and Sales Department; that, in turn, will allow you to have more powerful information from which to work. The right data will tell you, in very clear terms, where you need to put course correction into place well before problems show up on a profit and loss statement, thereby giving you more control over your future.

For Constantine, we used a Bid and Close Rate Tracking Tool (which you can download for free on my website at https://theprofitbleed.com/resources) to set estimating and close rate percentage goals that lined up with Constantine's revenue goals for the next twelve months. While they hadn't been tracking it on paper, Bruce and Scott's gut sense was that their historical close rate ran about thirty percent. They felt this was a good number to shoot for. They felt that if they could continue to get that close rate with the changes in pricing they'd implemented so far it would be a win. With a revenue goal of $15 million, they needed to bid $50 million worth of work ($15 million divided by 0.30 equals $50 million).

This simple piece promised to give a totally different shape to the estimating and sales process for Bruce. It would shift the game from one of "bid as much as you possibly can and hope for the best" to one of "bid and work the sales process to close enough sales to meet your revenue goals." This would allow two things to happen. One, it would give Bruce and Scott a goal, so they would know when they could stop "worrying" about sales; and two, it would give them metrics by which they could measure their effectiveness.

Once Bruce got comfortable with the Bid and Close Rate Tracking Tool, he could begin having his other estimators use it as well. We customized it to allow for all the estimators to start putting in their bid data in one sheet, which would allow Bruce to see each person's bidding volume and close rate percentages.

Each month, Bruce and Scott could sit together and enter how much they thought projects would bill each month, on the tracking backlog tab. At the bottom of the sheet they could see the total by month—with a row for their revenue goals, and the difference between projected and budget.

Once they began doing this, the Estimating Department would have a specific goal to work towards for meeting their revenue goal each month. This excited Scott as it would allow him to see staffing needs and know if his guys would have work in the coming months. If there was a lull coming up, it could be "all hands on deck" to fill the gap.

RESULTS SPEAK FOR THEMSELVES

Bruce and Scott left my office with a determination to try "Vicki's sales process." Now, as Bruce spends more time on the front end screening prospects and having in-depth conversations, he spends less time bidding and more time closing projects. As the partners have continued to work what they now consider "our sales process," they've seen continued improvements in their close rates and revenues.

PULSE POINTS

1. Put your sales process in writing (or write one) and insure it has questions and checklists that allow both you and the prospect to get a clear understanding of what's not working, and what they'd like. This process is not just about the data, it's about building a system that allows you and the prospect to have clarity, increase confidence, and build trust.
2. Establish sales and close rate percentage goals and track your results against those goals monthly.
3. Look at overall bid results every six months to a year and see if the people you are bidding to repeatedly are actually hiring you to do work, or just using you to get a price.

For tools and resources that will let you get your finger on the pulse of your business go to: https://theprofitbleed.com/resources

If you want to make a consistent profit...

you need to have a plan for controlling job costs. One that includes a clear hand-off process between Sales and Production, and the relentless management of labor hours.

CHAPTER 3

PRODUCTION

It's great to talk about profit margins and sales, but production is where the rubber meets the road. At our next meeting, Scott admitted that he often felt frustrated that foremen were not taking more ownership of projects.

"Just last week a foreman called me exasperated that the windows had not arrived, and his crew didn't have enough work to keep them busy for the day. Then he went on to say the painters were supposed to be priming the cabinets starting that day, and no one had shown up. 'Can you find out what's going on please so I can know what to tell my guys and the client about will be happening with the cabinets?'

"Calls like that are a daily event. I'd given the foreman all the project information, including subs and material orders. I don't know why it always comes down to the last minute like this. I've told them to verify deliveries and subs. They just never seem to get it done until the last minute."

Scott admitted that he often felt like a fire fighter. He couldn't see beyond the never-ending problems. He was frustrated and exhausted, and constantly running over budget on projects to boot. Scott had to do a lot of handholding with his guys. He expected the crews to know how to do the work—after all, he'd hired them for those skill sets.

If you have employees, you know that production is the place with the potential for not only the biggest headaches, but also the greatest loss and most risk. Part of the problem stems from a lack of project planning, which involves doing the front-end work to ensure that when the project is finished, the results are what you planned and you've not had to bolster it up along the way. Contractors often lose money when their people take on tasks outside of scope without a signed change order, or when hours run out on a line item before the work is completed. You can mitigate those risks by having a good project hand-off process with the field, along with a system for managing schedule milestones throughout the job: managing hours burned against budget, and a tightly managed, well-communicated, and strictly adhered to change order process.

As I said this, Bruce and Scott nodded their heads emphatically. "Oh yeah, we've struggled with exactly those issues," said Scott. "So often guys are doing work outside of the scope of what was bid, of what's in the plans, and we get a bunch of cost over-runs. I seem to always be scrambling to try and understand whether the work was due to our mistake, a client's request, a change in scope from the architect or designer, or simply an unforeseen glitch.

"In the past, few years, we've been doing more of the work ourselves and not subcontracting out things like framing, painting, and cabinet installation. We thought this approach would allow us to increase our profits as labor has higher markups on it then subcontractors. The problem, however, is that we've also seen that it takes a whole lot more to manage when we're dealing with our own crews. When we're working with a subcontractor, we also don't have the same risk—they're working from a fixed price. I can't do that with my employees."

I listened carefully. When faced with a problem, I'm always interested in knowing not just how to solve it, but also the *source* of it. What's the missing system, structure, process, or procedure that has allowed the train to come off the track in the first place? In the case of Constantine's production crew, I was certain the scope problem wasn't a result of them hiring lazy or stupid people—it rarely ever is.

So, the three of us went back to the basics. Scott, Bruce, and I came to a clear understanding that production is about three fundamental things: delivering on time, on budget, and as promised. This is the work of a contracting company at its core. Whatever systems they put into place needed to be in service of supporting that goal.

I asked Bruce what his current "hand-off process" from Sales to Production entailed.

THE HAND-OFF PROCESS

Bruce explained that, once a project contract was signed, he'd do a walkthrough with the foremen and then provide him with the estimate, which included figures for each phase, including hours. Bruce had been in business for years; he could eyeball most things. That, however, was the extent of their communication. The information was handed off in a somewhat casual fashion.

As I dug deeper, I also found that Bruce hadn't been documenting exclusions or assumptions in his estimates. Sure, he'd talked it through with the foremen on the walk-through, wasn't that enough? They were all professionals.

I suggested that Bruce do two things. "First, when doing an estimate, start documenting what is and is not included in the estimate, and what assumptions are being made. Begin writing more detailed notes in your bids for the foremen about what assumptions you've made, what is and is not included, specifying each with a callout. Second, start breaking down the hours more clearly in each phase or task of work by cost code."

"I get it about breaking out hours by cost code better, but shouldn't the foreman be writing down the other details when I do the walkthrough so they'll remember what I tell them? That will take a lot of time for me to document all that stuff," Bruce said.

Scott jumped in. He seemed a bit defensive about his department's lack of performance. "I expect the foremen to get the download from Bruce. I'm involved in the estimating phase of a project, as Bruce will run things by me. I have enough of the details to be able to project manage, and the field just needs to be more rigorous in taking notes when getting the download from Bruce. I can't do it all."

I realized at that moment that I needed to be mindful in how I was approaching this conversation with Bruce and Scott. The last thing I wanted to do was make them feel "wrong" and shut down. I went on.

"Given that one of the places where you've been burned is in change orders, don't you think it would make sense for you to give your team more clarity when it comes to job details? And documented job details are what you get when you have a good hand-off process. I appreciate it will take more time; however, investing here could make you a whole boatload more money on the bottom line when projects begin coming in on budget. It will allow Scott to stop babysitting, and get on to providing better service to clients and better managing the schedule. Both of which will get you more referrals."

> An effective hand-off process includes:
> - Clearly documented scope, assumptions and exclusions.
> - Budgeted dollars and hours by phase of work / cost code.
> - What subs are in contract, and which still need to be secured.
> - Any other unique issues around scope, job site, owners, other stakeholders, etc.

Scott looked relieved. The reality is that people hear the overall description of a project, then start working through the parts and pieces, and hope for the best when all is said and done. While we'd like to think the foreman will pour over the estimate and plans to make sure they're on track, it rarely happens that way. Without the details spelled out, without metrics from which to measure progress, there are no identifiable goals, nothing for the foremen to keep them on point with the budget and schedule.

Without a clear and detailed hand-off process from the Sales Department to the Production Department, the field crew will be handicapped in their ability to bring the project in on time and on budget, as promised. Part of this is due to people's inclination to do what they assume needs to be done next, and then deal with the next thing when it's presented. This lack of planning isn't malicious; it's simply that a lot of folks in construction don't naturally come with that skillset and need to be taught how to plan effectively.

An effective job hand-off process educates the team on the goals and objectives of a project. It provides the Production Department a clear roadmap that tells those involved what they are building, the planned scope and promised deliverables, the budget in dollars, and labor hours for each phase of work. It also informs them of what assumptions were made when figuring scope and cost, as well as what's NOT included in the project scope and budget.

If we were going to set Scott and his team up to be more successful on projects, and stop losing Constantine money, we needed an iron clad hand-off process, and a clearly documented change order process in place. Without a change order process, the scope of a project would continue to go unchecked.

There are many types of change orders, and it's a good to be clear about what these are with clients and your team *before* a project begins.

> Here is a list of potential areas where a change in price can occur:
> - Client initiated—the client requests additional work or the removal of work.
> - Client and architect initiated—the scope was not clearly defined in the original plans and added onto later.
> - Architect initiated—there are specification changes after the start of work.
> - Unforeseen conditions—there are changes due to the likes of dry rot, faulty wiring, or an unstable foundation.
>
> Your contracts should include a sheet explaining to a client the ways changes may occur, and your policy on how you will manage those changes throughout the project. One critical element here is that everyone agrees that work is not done out of scope without a signed change order or signed fieldwork authorization.

"Even with a good hand-off process," Scott said, "we don't trust that they'll own their projects the way you've described. How do we know they'd stop long enough to fill out a change order when they rarely do it now?"

Scott expounded upon this. "Listen, it's not like I don't tell them what to do. At the beginning of each week, we have a call and tell them what's coming up this week, and what work should occur to keep us on schedule, on budget."

Most business owners would like to believe that, just because they hire people who have done a job before, no further supervision is required. Employees, particularly those with experience, should just do what they've been asked, without all the "babysitting."

The problem, I explained, was not entirely with the foremen. The real issue is that the foremen are not told exactly what they are accountable for (in the form of a job description) and are not held accountable in any real way for managing the *results* of a project. They get a pass on cost overruns and missed deadlines.

"You may be able to make them accountable for doing the layout and physical work, but you've got to assume the rest of the responsibility lies with you, Scott. Without systems and tools (like a good hand-off process), and insistence on people following your change order process, that's all but impossible. You simply don't have enough bandwidth to do that effectively, as you already know."

We ended our meeting with an agreement: Bruce promised to document projects with more detail and spend more time during the hand-off process. He also agreed to write up a detailed procedure of the hand-off process and run it by Scott to get his input. Once that was done, he would implement it starting with the next signed project. Scott agreed to write up and implement a tight change order process. He agreed to be the one to present their policy on change orders in the client meetings and would train the foremen on it as well.

PROGRESS IS MADE

The following month as we began our meeting, Bruce shared that he had discovered, much to his delight, the process of documenting his thinking and approach to the estimate had provided *him* more clarity. He was more confident about what needed to be included in prices, and in scope. He found that handing off projects to the field, while taking more time, felt more complete; and the foremen seemed to really appreciate the additional detail.

Then Scott jumped in, telling me about how he'd written up their change order policy and implemented it with clients and the field. He was already starting to see more change orders coming in.

I was impressed with how Bruce and Scott had worked to iron out the hand-off process and the management of change orders.

THE TWO-WEEK LOOK-AHEAD

When they finished sharing the progress they'd made, I congratulated them both and asked Scott if the dynamic between him and the foremen had changed.

"While they're doing well with capturing more change orders, and seem to be more aware of job scope, they still don't seem to have control of their projects. I am still getting persistent and never-ending calls. Clearly, something is still missing."

The look on his face was one of frustration and even anger.

"Let's talk about what you need to have in place with the foremen to eliminate the persistent calling, the never-ending urgent needs and requests that come to you at all hours of the day."

As we began exploring his current process, Scott explained that he was the conduit for all sub scheduling, ordering of materials, and interfacing with clients. I pointed out that there was no way the company could grow if he continued to be the one that controlled all those pieces. He took a deep breath as he shook his head in agreement. "That's an understatement," he said.

I explained that successful contracting companies have their foremen do a lot of those things, and then report back to the operations manager bi-weekly on results. "If you continue to be the conduit for all that information, then you'll continue to be a fireman."

"But I'm worried about losing control of the project," said Scott with a panicked look on his face. I could sense Scott's hesitation—this is how he's always done it, and doing it differently is scary.

"Do you really have control now?" I asked.

"No, not really. I mostly feel like I'm doing CPR on a project. I'm always chasing after the next bleeder that needs to be stopped."

"Exactly! That's why you want to learn to delegate those things and manage results, versus micro manage the particles and pieces. You'll want to set up a system whereby the foremen are doing their own planning and looking ahead on projects, tracking material orders, scheduling subs, and meeting with clients on job progress. Your job is then to review with them, every two weeks, where the project is currently and where it is headed for the next two weeks."

I wanted him to understand that proactively looking ahead on jobs allows him to plan more effectively and set expectations with the rest of the team and subcontractors. Everyone is on the same page then, and the foremen has more control over results. Scott already knew that not staying in front of production caused cost overruns, work inefficiencies, and resentment from subs for lack of planning—not to mention constantly fighting fires.

Scott nodded in agreement. "So, what's the tool?" he asked.

"Doing a two-week look-ahead process on all projects. It's a tool that allows the foremen to plan the next two weeks. It includes identifying milestones, material needs, the need to schedule subs, and future and open requests for information and submittal. On the form is also an area where any issues or concerns with the project can be noted, any items that need to be communicated to the office can be spelled out, and any client issues that need to be addressed can be outlined.

"Let me share a story about my client Joe," I said. "Joe had been facing some of the same challenges you're facing. When Joe implemented the two-week look-ahead process it was clunky at first. Even though Joe had trained his foremen on how to use the form, they were not used to having to think and plan in this way. For several weeks, the foremen would show up to the meetings with blank forms. Over time, Joe trained them to see the two-week look-ahead to make their lives easier, and to help them feel like they were more in control of how projects flowed. Within a few months, there were less urgent calls coming into Joe each day. The foremen began showing up to meetings with the form filled out, and asking more questions. They began having more clarity about the trajectory of their projects, and thus, more confidence about what they needed to do to keep it on track.

"As the urgent calls to Joe became fewer and fewer, he started spending more time on managing the big picture of projects—scheduling, and projecting financially where the job would end up. Joe started doing the job of a project manager—insuring projects came in on time, on budget, as promised. Added benefit? Joe started enjoying his work more, and spent less time at the office. The foremen were also happier, and liked feeling like they had more control over the jobs they managed."

I could tell by the look on Scott's face as he sat up straight, he liked the idea. There was a glimmer of hope and even excitement in his eyes as the prospect of no longer being a fire fighter started to look like a real possibility.

"I'm going to encourage you to be patient with the process." I said. "It takes time for people to learn new behavior, and I want to encourage you to keep in mind that your job here is to build great foremen, not just teach a task. Building great foremen will serve you and them better in the long-run, just as it did Joe. So be consistent and keep working the tool until it's really solid—this could take several months."

> When you're clear about where you're headed you have more control, and a better chance of having projects come in on time, on budget, as promised. Clarity produces confidence, and confidence allows you to take more thoughtful and powerful actions. Doing two-week look-ahead allows you to do this.

PULSE POINTS

1. Have a tight change order process in place that ensures you don't do work out of scope without prior client authorization. This can be signed field work authorizations and change orders. Review these on jobs at least once a month with foreman and/or project manager.
2. Have foremen and project managers review hours burned against budget reports every week and work out a plan for staying on budget, and/or identify where change orders are needed.
3. Do project two-week look-ahead reports every two weeks and clearly spell out the next two-week critical milestone actions and plan.

For tools and resources that will let you get your finger on the pulse of your business go to:
https://theprofitbleed.com/resources

If you want to make a consistent profit...

you need to set company goals for how much profit you want to make. Then you need to get consistent, accurate, timely feedback that lets you keep your finger on the pulse of where you are in relationship to those goals.

CHAPTER 4

FEEDBACK

I knew some of the heavy lifting was still in front of us. In our next meeting, we needed to continue to work through the core source of Constantine's problems: why they were losing money. Improving pricing, having a sales process, and setting up systems and procedures for the hand-off into Production were great first steps. A two-week look-ahead that allowed the foremen to take ownership and have more control over the results of their projects was one more victory the company was beginning to enjoy. But a few key elements still needed to be dealt with, the first of which was getting better feedback systems in place.

FEEDBACK

Plain and simple, we needed more from the foremen. If Bruce and Scott wanted their foremen to be successful in production, the partners needed feedback from them on a consistent basis. The kind of feedback, we'll get into in a bit.

I also knew that if Bruce and Scott were not looking at their financial results on a regular basis, they would continue to run their company in the dark—which is how they had arrived at the state of affairs they were in when we first met.

Both the detailed feedback from the foremen and the big-picture feedback from the Finance Department were vital to the health of the business.

It was apparent, when we first began our work together, the feedback Constantine was getting from the Finance Department was sorely lacking. It had taken several weeks for the bookkeeper to provide the reports for me to do my initial Financial Health Assessment.

Beyond the snail's pace response, the data that was finally delivered didn't allow me, or anyone else for that matter, to decipher Constantine's true gross profit margin. I had to dig for it, run a few calculations, to pull up a number that should have been easily identifiable.

To make matters worse, it was taking two to three months for Bruce and Scott to get vital financial reports; and because they'd all but given up on banking on data, job cost reports were rarely reviewed by Scott, the foremen, or anybody else. We've clearly established that not reviewing the numbers is bad, particularly when they represent a pulse point. Today we were going to address all that.

I began our latest meeting by asking Bruce and Scott about the schedule they had set up with accounting for producing job cost reports and monthly financial statements. While I pretty much knew the answer, I didn't want to appear presumptuous.

They looked at one another, then at me, and shrugged. "Whenever we get them I guess," replied Scott.

"And do you feel like the feedback you're getting is providing you with a clear picture of where you're at on projects?"

"No, not really. We're always so busy marketing, selling, bidding, and taking care of clients that we don't have much time."

By the look they shot each other, I could see that they felt ridiculous.

The reason most contractors are chained to their business twenty-four/seven is the fear that things will fall apart the minute they walk offsite, even for a minute. They don't trust that surprise glitches can be handled without their input, and they can sense these glitches lurking in the shadows. At any minute, a project will get delayed, or run way off budget—then where will they be? If you're a contractor, your opportunity to get away from your business, with the confidence that it's working well without you, is completely dependent on your ability to manage by results, and manage from the whole versus the particles and pieces.

A critical element in being able to deliver projects on time, and on budget is immediate access to feedback that allows you to see where you are each week against job budget so you can make immediate course corrections where needed. Without good reporting, without consistent, regular review of feedback by both you and your team, catching mistakes before they take the legs out from under you is nearly impossible. These glitches do not need to surprise you.

Of course, it would be easy to blame your financial people for the lack of critical data. Yet the first step in the process involves you. You've got to get information into accounting in a timely and accurate manner, and then set a schedule for the generation of feedback reports. Your staff will not do this without a procedure.

THE DATA

People often consider accounting a necessary evil to get bills paid, payroll issued, and billings sent out. While they definitely perform all of these functions, this department is also a critical conduit of information for your company. Small businesses often miss this fact.

The Finance Department is probably the most overlooked, underutilized resource in a small business. Their work product is considered predictable, repetitive, and mundane. Yet, these very qualities disguise the department's hidden power. Buried in the mundane is the unvarnished truth. Buried in the thousands of figures at their fingertips are the pulse points of the business's health.

It's amazing how often business owners lack a clear plan for the generation of data that will allow them to see the numbers for what they really are. Financial reports are the lifeblood to providing vital feedback. Feedback, the right feedback, will give you clarity—where you were yesterday; where you are today; where you're headed tomorrow. That clarity will allow you to take more powerful actions. That clarity will also allow you to cut surprises off at the pass, so you can step away from the office long enough to take a break, or even a real vacation.

The truth is, when you learn to manage by results using the feedback you get, not only from accounting, but also from estimating, sales, and production, you'll find yourself far less stressed; you'll know when you can stop worrying. You'll also know where you need to push on sales, production, and profitability. The right reporting feedback is the key to your freedom, peace of mind, and profitability.

As I was explaining this concept to Bruce and Scott, they sat a little straighter and scooted up in their chairs as I spoke. I could tell by the look on their faces that what I was saying was registering for them in an entirely new way.

"We like that idea of having less stress and more peace of mind," said Scott.

"So, what's the trick to getting better and more timely feedback?" asked Bruce. "And what feedback should we be looking at exactly?"

"Good questions. Let me explain."

We'd talked about the sales pipeline and close rate reporting, and worked on two-week look-ahead planning with the foremen, now it was time to dig a little deeper into the accounting side. The more planned your Finance Department functions are, and the quicker you get feedback that shows results on projects, not to mention your company, the sooner you can put course corrections in place, and positively affect the bottom line. The longer you wait, the harder it is to make course corrections, and the more money you can potentially lose. Information isn't just power, it's money.

First, let's talk about the timing of getting information into your accounting system, and then what job and financial reports you'll want to be looking at.

YOUR ACCOUNTING CALENDAR

The solution to timely reporting is to have an accounting calendar that identifies what tasks are performed and when. For instance, payroll is done on Mondays and Tuesdays; payables are entered on Thursdays; check runs are done on Fridays; receivable billings are done every other Wednesday, and all data entry is completed by the end of each week, including posting of any hand cut checks. This ensures that on Monday morning you can run up-to-date job reports. Included in the accounting calendar is a month end close process whereby other monthly accounting entries are made, such as recurring journal entries, work in progress adjustments, accruals, and any other adjusting entries. Your goal should be to have books closed and company financial reports produced by the tenth of each month.

    Bruce looked a little sheepish. His eyes were cast down. "That would be great, but I've gotta tell ya, when I get those reports, I'm never really sure what I'm looking for. It's one of the reasons I avoid looking at them in the first place."

    This issue had come up in one of our first meetings, and now was the perfect time to take the conversation to the next level.

    "Totally OK. We all have to begin somewhere."

I've seen this so often over the years: business owners who don't know how to read their own financial reports, who get intimated by the numbers. Some don't look at them because it looks like a straight up foreign language; some don't look at them because they know the results don't look all that great, and they figure it's easier to just not look at all.

There's a book by Jim Collins, titled *Good to Great*, about a multi-year study he and his team did to identify the characteristics of great companies and leaders. Each chosen company had to be in business for fifteen years or longer, had to have faced major breakdown that they overcame, and had to out-perform the market at least six times. The final list of "great" companies that met these criteria, as well as others, totaled thirteen. Most of them were names you wouldn't recognize. When Collins interviewed the CEOs of these companies, he bumped into something interesting. One of the consistent traits each possessed, across the board, was their willingness to "confront the brutal facts." They treated the feedback of the business as a tool to help them become better leaders, not as something they needed to be embarrassed by or ashamed of. They used the feedback to make course corrections and grow their companies.

Their basic philosophy? If you can *see* what the issues are, then you can do something about them.

The same should be true for you in your business. Whether the numbers are what you want them to be or not, they're a powerful tool to help you grow your company. Your reports are the control panel that let you manage the whole of your company, even when you're sitting in a beach chair.

I explained to Bruce and Scott that we'd review their financial reports together each month and I'd show them how to read and use them the way one would any powerful tool. But for now, I'd come at the problem from an angle they could more easily understand.

And what these partners understood had to do with individual jobs and the need for reporting.

REPORTING

Project (and financial) reports are the key to keeping your finger on the pulse of your company's health. I've said that before and I'll say it again. When you review them on a regular basis, you'll start to see where the gap exists between your actual results and your desired results. This gives you the ability to focus on those areas and come up with a plan of action for making corrections.

It's important to understand that numbers in and of themselves don't mean anything. They only mean something in relationship to something else. (And this goes beyond the whole feeling afraid to look at your numbers because they're proof of personal failure.)

For example: when you're looking at an hour burned report for a project—that data means something in relationship to budgeted hours, and the job schedule. If you've used seventy-five percent of the hours and you're not even halfway through the job, you're going to have to figure out where things went amiss in the budget or on that schedule. When you're looking at the financial reports for your company, they mean something in relationship to the goals you set, industry averages, and prior year's performance. It's not about the number itself, but where you are in relation to the bar you're paying attention to; that's where the shortfall lies.

I leaned in closer to Bruce and Scott. "So, let's talk about some of the key numbers you want to look at for your projects. You know that a project in and of itself won't make or break you, but a whole series of them can."

PROJECT REPORTING

The key focus of project management is to keep projects on time, on budget, and ensure delivery as promised. We talked about this in the last chapter. Unfortunately, being the manager of said projects can sometimes feel more like being a fire fighter, as Scott was so fond of saying. Life had gotten easier for Scott since he implemented the two-week look-ahead reporting. That was the first step, but now accounting would need to provide the foremen with additional feedback, so they could measure how they were doing, tell if they were on track or not. Scott would need to become skilled at project reporting, which would be possible once Bruce and Scott put a schedule in place that ensured accurate and up-to-date data. If the partners understood the big picture, they would act accordingly.

There are a few key reports Scott would need to go over with his foremen every other week. I pointed out that the best reports to start with would be job hours burned against budgeted hours; committed costs report by cost code with budget; committed costs remaining; actual cost-to-date; and percent complete. Depending on the size of a job, these reports could be reviewed weekly.

On my website, I have a full list of suggested project reports to review, including recommended timeframes for when to review them, and it's free. Check out "Reports for Management" at https://theprofitbleed.com/resources. It will provide pointers on what to look for as well.

Right away, Scott and his foremen would see the benefit of looking at the job as a whole versus just the day-to-day particles and pieces - you know, all those things that pull at your attention each day. The details of the subcontractor schedule; the pricing for a change order; the delivery of materials; or the tracking of employee time. While these are all important, your ability to control the success of a project is dependent upon looking at the whole of all those parts and making course corrections to keep the project on track.

Putting their heads together, both the foremen and Scott would be able to have conversations about where there were potential overruns in costs, and/or potential savings. The foremen could start using the hour report to plan the hours to complete various tasks with their team. Over time, jobs would start coming in on time, and on budget more consistently.

Clarity about job-results-to-date and compared budgets allows everyone involved to have faith that the project will go as planned. They'll stop looking over their shoulders waiting for the other shoe to drop. There's nothing better than knowing where a project will end up before it's history.

Now it was time for me to broaden the picture. I would need to step lightly because of the fear factor.

"We all understand when a project goes off budget, but what happens when you're unaware of where you stand as a company? What happens when you don't know if you've deviated from what you can actually afford to spend?"

Bruce and Scott looked nervous.

I took a deep breath and launched into two of the most important types of feedback tools: the operating budget and variance reporting.

OPERATING BUDGET

Here's one of the few commands I will give you; it's that important: Do an operating budget and track your results against it each month.

An operating budget, much like a project budget, lets you make a plan. Tracking your results against that plan allows you to know if you're going to meet your profit goals, and if not, where you need to make course corrections. Without a guidepost to direct you, which is what your budget is, you'll just keep working harder and harder hoping it will all turn out, which in the long run, just exhausts you, and everyone involved.

The partners at Constantine Contracting rolled their eyes the first time I mentioned doing an operating budget for their company.

"Worried it'll be too constricting?" I asked.

"It's just that any time we've attempted to do a budget for our company it's just ended up being a wild-ass guess about what we're going to do, and then it never gets looked at again."

The partners at Constantine are not alone. So often people think putting together a budget is a waste of time because they equate it with simply sitting down in front of a spreadsheet, throwing numbers on the page, and calling it good. My approach to budgeting is *not* that.

An operating budget should be a roadmap for helping you navigate your way to a successful result. In fact, it's no different than a well-planned-out project budget. You start out knowing you have certain goals for the margins you want to make, you look at the resources you'll need to get the job done, and you spend time planning how you will build the project. Think of an operating budget as a project budget for your company. This time, a healthy company is your project.

> Operating budgets are a great way to create a plan and set goals for what you want to do for the year. If you want to see profit, you can't skip the planning and the thinking through process. You can't shy away from precision and detail because they're key. We have a budget template tool that walks you through creating your operating budget—feel free to check it out.
> https://suiterbusinessbuilders.com/tools/templates/

As Bruce, Scott and I worked on an operating budget for the year, they set goals for bidding and sales against which Bruce would track results.

By the fifteenth of each month, they would review actual results against budget, analyzing where they were and were not meeting their targets. They would look at where there were variances in overhead costs, where there were trends in revenue variances (looking at the month, quarter, and year-to-date side by side).

This is how Scott and Bruce would begin managing the "whole of their business;" this is how they would gain a greater power to know what course corrections they needed to make to meet their profitability goals. Not just project by project, but company-wide.

■ ■ ■

Again, numbers in and of themselves don't mean anything, I explained. Have data to compare your results to; this is what will give your numbers more meaning. For example, a profit and loss compared to budget will tell you where you are compared to your plan. Looking at this year versus last year profit and loss and balance sheet numbers will tell you how your results compare to the prior year. As you begin looking at the data, the numbers will start to tell you a story about your company's health and performance.

If you'd like more help reading your financial reports, look on my website for your free resource titled "How to Read Your Financial Reports" at https://theprofitbleed.com/resources.

Here's another huge benefit—as you begin meeting your goal, you'll find yourself breathing a sigh of relief. When your margins are on track with your targets, you'll relax into your office chair knowing you're on track. When there's a variance, you'll know where to look to find more answers. If revenue is off, you'll look to your sales tracking worksheet and backlog report to check for timing issues, or if there's a potential you won't meet your revenue goals for the year. If expenses are over, you'll be able to identify which ones are over and, upon closer examination, see if an unexpected cost, careless spending, or even a potential error cropped up. The numbers will start to have more meaning because you now have something to compare the data to. They'll tell you where to look for the issues.

And when you know where the issues are, you can fix them.

FINAL THOUGHTS

When you have a plan against which to evaluate your results, your numbers will have more meaning. When you have greater clarity regarding where you are in relation to your plan, you will have more confidence in knowing what actions to take to put course correction in place. This is how you stay in front of your numbers. This is how you increase your profitability, both on jobs and for your company: you manage results—on a regular schedule, against a plan, faithfully. This is the key to your peace of mind, and the ticket to your freedom: have a plan and manage your results, consistently, against that plan.

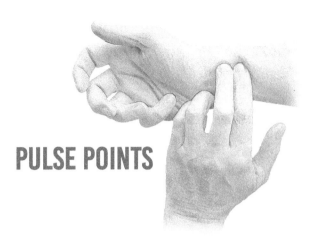

PULSE POINTS

1. At the beginning of each year, establish an operating budget that plans for the desired profits you want to make.
2. Have an accounting calendar in place that ensures all project data is up to date by end of the day each Friday, and then manage to those deadlines.
3. Compare actual results to budget each month, with reports to management ideally by the 15th of each month. Read those reports and review key numbers: revenue, gross profit margin, and net profit margin against goal.
4. Review balance sheet ratios each month to assess the financial health of your company overall.

For tools and resources that will let you get your finger on the pulse of your business go to: https://theprofitbleed.com/resources

If you want to make a consistent profit...

you need to be rigorous in managing project schedules and client expectations. That includes knowing where the project's final dollars will land well in advance of the project end date – for both you and the client.

CHAPTER 5

PROJECT MANAGEMENT

Over the next few months, Bruce, Scott, and I sat down with their thirty-day financial results for the prior month, quarter, and year-to-date—profit and loss statement, actual results compared to budget, as well as the balance sheet for the period—and a trend appeared. The gross profit margin, while improved over the year before, was not meeting their budget goals. The partners were visibly upset. They'd changed a number of things: how they were pricing and marking up projects when bidding; how they managed the hand-off process from sales to production; how they insisted the foremen do two-week look-ahead reporting. As a result, they expected stronger results. They expected a higher profit margin.

I explained to Scott and Bruce that there were four primary culprits usually at play:

Projects were estimated at a lower margin than the company goals.

There was cost overruns on projects in production.

Changes in scope were not being captured in change orders (resulting in cost overruns).

Billings were not being done on a consistent basis.

The two men thought for a moment. Bruce was estimating at targeted gross profit margins, he said as much. He understood how important that was to do after our very first come-to-Jesus meeting; and he confirmed that accounting was up to date on billings because he'd made sure of it. That left the problem in production as cost overruns, or change orders not being captured.

> To understand what's driving your contracting company's profitability, you need to dig down to job level, so you can see which specific projects are driving your overall results. Tracking production costs by job will allow you to get this level of feedback.

Clearly, this was the time for Scott and me to talk about project management best practices. Up until now, we'd only discussed the various places in production to manage results. This base had given Scott and his foremen greater focus of what actions to take to stay on top of production, but most of that was short-term.

"You and your foremen have done a great job in putting a tight change order process in place, and implementing the two-week look-ahead reporting to allow projects to run more smoothly, and keep the company from losing money on change orders. The next thing to tackle is managing projects from a big picture perspective. We want to think in terms of the long haul, right through to the end of production."

There was one final piece to put in place before we could do this: doing cost to complete projections each month. This practice is better than a crystal ball for determining what the financial future holds. Cost to complete is a forecast or estimated prediction that includes both objective (science) and subjective (art) elements.

"There's a key," I continued. "We need to see where projects are heading well in advance of the results occurring. We need to get out in front of problems, not wait for them to happen."

Scott looked confused. "There are so many things to manage on a project—costs, customer relations, material procurement, subcontractors, scheduling guys, requests for changes, submittals, and requests for information. It's a lot to juggle. I mean, I'm starting to see how the foremen doing the two-week look-ahead are helping to control the chaos, but in many ways, I still feel like I'm chasing after stuff and fighting fires every day. Are you saying there's *more* to do?"

"Not more," I said, knowing how the very idea of additional reporting and analysis would make anybody feel, myself included. "Simply a planned approach to address when and how you'll deal with all those elements. Establishing a sort of briefing process in which you identify the most probable obstacles and glitches; then outlining a strategy to deal with them. I'm talking about getting control of projects so you're not just reacting, but become more proactive."

Getting control and managing projects for the long term—through the end of production—and using established tools to allow you to do this, that's the real job of a project manager.

The key elements to a planned approach: tight schedules with milestones and deadlines; projecting cost to complete; regularly scheduled site visits; regularly scheduled client and team meetings; and reviewing job reports regularly. These are the established tools of an effective project manager.

"What am I missing then?" said Scott. "I think I'm doing all those things."

"Let me ask you this. When you look at the declining profit margins on projects, do you know what specific jobs are causing that drop, and do you have a plan to stop the bleed?"

Scott shook his head no.

"If you don't know which organ is bleeding, how will you know how to keep the patient alive and well?"

TIGHT SCHEDULES

Let me share with you another story about my client, Joe (we spoke about him earlier.) He'd implemented the two-week look-ahead I'd recommended, but he too noticed that jobs weren't coming in at the estimated gross profit margin. As we talked it through, and looked at the data, it became clear that Joe wasn't working from a master schedule for projects. The somewhat informal schedule that he did have wasn't being updated on a consistent basis. He wasn't tightly managing milestones, thus wasn't clear what had to be done next to avoid predictable issues. This proved to be a problem. I encouraged him to start doing project schedules that were updated every two weeks with clearly defined milestones. Which would then line up with the cycle for when he was meeting with clients. That way, he could assess the full scope of the project, as it currently existed, including all changes, and all factors that had impacted the schedule along the way.

> When scheduling, it's important to identify milestones that will drive other production deadlines such as customer selections, ordering of materials, or specialty items. Including labor resources as an overlay on a schedule is also a great way to simultaneously manage staffing needs, which are notoriously problematic.

As Joe started using well-thought-out schedules as the focal point for regular foremen meetings, he saw his foremen begin to engage in the bigger picture and end results of their projects. They started to really grasp the trajectory they needed to be on to deliver the promise of "on time" and "on budget." There were no more excuses for time delays because cabinets hadn't been ordered when they should have been; there was no longer the need bring in a subcontractor to solve a sudden problem.

GET CONTROL OF THE PROJECT

As project manager, Joe also began to work on better job planning. He focused on things like team meetings, client meetings, the review of reports, site visits, and projecting project costs through completion (we'll talk about this in a minute). He began to understand that his very job as project manager needed to be thought of like a project schedule. It wasn't always exact, he had to play some things by ear, but if he set milestones and deadlines on his own calendar, he could dramatically increase the odds of his projects turning out as planned.

Well-controlled project management planning includes:

Reviewing reports and feedback, and doing projections on a regularly scheduled basis. Having a specific day / time each week when this will be done.

Conducting project meetings with the key players once a week or every other week at a pre-scheduled time.

Updating and discussing open items with the client at a consistent, scheduled time each week.

Going over job results and open issues to be addressed with your foremen at a scheduled time every other week. This would address schedule, two-week look-ahead, and labor hours burnt reporting.

Obviously, timeframes will vary depending on the size of your project. The point is: have a plan, and work your plan. Be consistent about it. If you don't have control of your jobs, they will have control of you. That's exhausting and frustrating, and will have you bleeding profits.

When Joe started doing well-thought-out schedules, and tightly managing milestones, projects started to see a dramatic increase in production efficiency, which translated to better profit margins.

As I shared this story with Scott, he wrote notes furiously. He said, "I'm starting to see your point. Get in front of it, schedule it out, plan it, and then, when the 'unexpected' happens, I'll be better prepared to deal with it. I'm taking control of the project rather than simply reacting to all of the disparate elements, and hoping I have time to get to everything."

"Exactly," I said. "And then you're not being a fire fighter; you're leading. Extra bonus: you'll find that you have more fun, and more time because *you* dictated the schedule."

"Maybe I'll be able to schedule that bike trip, too. Wouldn't that be great."

"The final step," I said, "is to use the information you're getting from the foremen in the two-week look-ahead, feedback from your meetings with the team (staff and subs), along with cost-to-date and committed cost reports, to start doing projected costs to complete each month. See how these pieces all fit together, how they build on one another as they click in place?"

PROJECTING TO THE END, COST TO COMPLETE PROJECTING

I reminded the partners of the key elements of Joe's story, the whole reason I was sharing it with them. While Joe saw an improvement in gross profits—after establishing a clear and thorough hand-off process from estimating, tighter project schedules, two-week look-ahead reporting, a better change order process, and having regular and consistent meetings with all the key players on a job—he was still seeing slippage in gross profit margin. Like everybody else, he felt like he just couldn't get it right, that the universe was conspiring against him. This was precisely how Scott and Bruce felt.

Just as I was doing with Scott and Bruce, I examined the specific cost line items that were running over with Joe. There were quite of few of them. In particular, he wasn't controlling costs on line items where there was labor creep. I also noticed that Joe wasn't projecting out the total cost for his and the foreman's time when submitting change orders.

I suggested Joe begin doing cost to complete projections each month that would have him and the other project managers looking at each cost code line, then identifying what they would spend on each by the time the project was complete. This required doing some calculating on labor hours and days to determine cost remaining for labor, as well as identifying where there was scope creep, or savings that were not in a change order. It also allowed them to see in advance where potential change order requests were needed. Fifteen minutes of calculation revealed ten red flags.

> Projecting costs to complete is looking at a project in real time, and estimating the total cost to finish the project. Starting with cost-to-date compared to budget along with committed costs will show you the budgeted dollars remaining (that which is not already spent or committed). The largest variable is always labor, which therefore needs detailed attention. Projecting hours to complete will help you get a handle on this.

As Joe and his project managers started doing cost to complete projections, they found they could more closely control the final cost on projects, and hit targeted final gross profit margins. They started to see where there were problems or potential cost overruns before they got ugly, so they could ask for more money in change orders, or work with their foremen to better control costs. Joe felt better, and so did his customers.

With this information in hand, Joe could project profitability for the company month to month. Gross profit margins started to show more consistency, as did the bottom line profitability of the company—which, if you recall, is the goal of the whole exercise.

Doing over/under billings each month, where you take into account projected over and under budget amounts on projects, provide you even more in-depth feedback on your company's actual earned revenue and gross profit margins to date. You should talk with your CPA about how to do this correctly.

While sharing Joe's story with the partners, I watched as Scott continued to take copious notes. In our meetings, I could tell he was really grasping this whole idea of managing the key drivers in each area of their company, and that this final piece on project management would help him get a better handle on where he should be focusing his time.

IN SUMMARY

By tightly managing schedules, milestones and deadlines, and having a grounded approach to managing budget by doing projected cost to complete, you will have more confidence about when projects will finish and what the total costs will be. The biggest benefit is this: you will have better control over project final gross profit margins. Having this kind of certainty allows you to communicate with the client about job progress and projected completion dates, and to justify the need for additional funds when they request changes.

A plan that's "worked" let's you feel like *you're* in control. No more wondering how and when all of those tasks and open items you're juggling will be addressed. This will then free up your brain to focus on more creative and strategic ways to keep a project on time, on budget, and as promised.

Over the next few months Scott began "working his plan" as a project manager, and focusing more and more time to managing schedule, client management, and doing monthly cost to completes on all their open projects. The outcome was more control over project results.

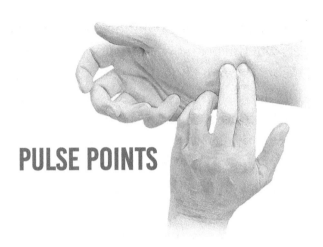

PULSE POINTS

1. Update project schedules every two weeks with milestones, deadlines, and labor/sub resources identified, and work out a plan for meeting those milestones.
2. Plan out all client, team, and site visit meetings at least two weeks in advance. Be consistent and rigorous in keeping to these schedules.
3. Have a specific date each month to review job reports (with foreman or superintendent if applicable). These include overall job progress, open change orders, RFI's, submittals and client issues. Create a plan to resolve.

4. By the fifth of each month, project cost to complete on all open projects - where you may be over or under budget. If over, is there a correction that needs to be made, or a change order processed?

For tools and resources that will let you get your finger on the pulse of your business go to: https://theprofitbleed.com/resources

If you want to make a consistent profit...

analyze your entire business operations and identify where you want to make improvements.

CHAPTER 6

TAKE AN EAGLE'S EYE VIEW OF YOUR BUSINESS

I'm going to repeat the exact same line I used in the introduction because it's so clear: if you follow the system and strategies I've laid out for you in this book, you'll regain control. You'll enjoy the byproduct of your efforts, something you may not have experienced in a very long time. Hey, maybe you'll even take some time off, have dinner with your family, get back to the gym, read a novel, and have more fun in life. All work and no play makes Jack a dull boy. It's time to get interesting again, to live.

Constantine Contracting? Well, they went from that loss of $250,000 three years before to a profit of over $1 million this past year, and they only grew $2 million more in revenues. That means they did fewer projects (in fact they got very selective), and they made far more profit.

Bruce and Scott each took a two-week vacation this past year, without a laptop, without calling in, or checking emails. They trusted that their team had business covered, that the systems they'd put in place had clued them into potential problems before they ever got on a plane. One week, they were both gone for a few days at the same time when a major problem arose. Their foreman handled it beautifully.

No longer do the partners work weekends, or get those frantic calls from upset customers on a

Saturday night. Bruce tells me he's back to riding his bike on weekends; and Scott has been racing again, which he'd put on the back shelf a few years back, figuring he'd never get back to it again.

The fact that they can enjoy an expanse of time without that non-stop feeling that a shoe is about to drop is probably the one thing they value most. Or maybe it's that they've started to build cash reserves, and are now debt free.

Bruce claims he's finding the entire sales process much more fun now that he's clearly grounded in the numbers. When a customer says, "It's too much," he loves being able to get creative, find acceptable ways to reduce costs. He reexamines scope and finds ways to help the client knock off a big chunk of change and still get what the client wants without finding fault with Constantine—a luxury Bruce never could have experienced before. He found that customers love having clear choices, a sense that they're standing at the control panel with him, not being taken advantage of. Customer paranoia has seemingly disappeared.

Scott is feeling confident in his field staff. His foremen now call him more to brainstorm instead of reporting on the crisis of the hour, which he always had to solve. He's feeling a greater sense of control over each and every project, not waiting for one of them to go rogue. Now that he's found more time to invest in visiting job sites, and engaging with clients, he deals with happier people and more quality leads.

Bruce and Scott have found the "sweet spot" of running their business. Things still break down from time to time, that's life, but they're no longer operating in crisis mode. They look at mishaps as opportunities for improvement. This mindset has given them both much more peace of mind about the future of their company.

One more thing: Scott and Bruce are making more, personally, from the business now than they ever have, and they're no longer afraid to take their draws in fear of compromising their bottom line.

Scott is dating again, now that he's recovered from the divorce. Bruce has lost nearly thirty pounds. Their faces are lighter these days, and their demeanor is clearly more relaxed. They like working with each other and their staff, and it shows.

Hundreds of other clients I've worked with are also generating consistent profits, working less, and having more fun in their businesses. That's what they wanted; that's why they hired me. All it took was getting clear about the numbers they needed to manage, and then consistently managing them.

Don't forget, management involves communicating with the team, and creating solid systems and processes to support everyone, to make them more successful in their jobs. Management doesn't mean coming up with some target numbers and sticking them in the drawer because you think they're pie in the sky, or useless.

As the cliché goes, my clients stopped simply working harder, and started working smarter. They set goals for what they wanted to achieve, and they consistently managed against those goals, and consistently looked for ways to increase efficiency and effectiveness in what they do. Notice the word *consistently*.

Of course, not all numbers are created equal. In fact, deal with too many numbers, and you'll probably drown.

We've discussed the key drivers to help you get control of the profits in your company, so you can have more time in your day. We've explored the pulse points my clients have learned to keep their finger on so they can outsmart trouble before it eats away their bottom line, and in the process, their very soul. We've pinpointed the numbers to track that would allow them to find more joy in their work, and a greater sense of clarity and confidence in their ability to create the success they so desire.

- So, how do you take this information, these tools and strategies, and apply them to your own business?
- How do you figure out where your company is leaking profits?
- How do you determine where the lack of systems is causing you way too much work?
- And where do you begin?

The first step is to assess your own business, analyze your own company. I encourage you to do this with your partners and/or your senior management team. You can download a free editable version of my "Business Health Assessment" worksheet at https://theprofitbleed.com/resources. This assessment tool gives you the questions and guidelines to follow to assess the health of your company, to determine where your company is bleeding profits, and to help you identify what actions you can take to make it healthy.

TAKE YOUR OWN PULSE-POINT ASSESSMENT

Wait, we've got time. That's what this book is all about, after all. Let's walk through this, step by step, key driver by key driver. Here are the important questions you'll ask yourself as you work through this Business Health Assessment, key area by key area.

PRICING (ESTIMATING)

- Do I know my real burdened cost for labor, and do my estimated costs take inflation into account when projects will occur more than six months out?
- Do I know my company's overhead breakeven percentage? Have I marked up my direct costs to cover this?
- Am I clear about my gross profit margin goal on projects? Do I mark up bids a sufficient amount to reach that goal? Check out the free downloadable "Markup and Margin Chart" to help you easily identify this amount at https://theprofitbleed.com/resources
- Do I consistently check bid overall profit before sharing it with prospects? Have I ensured we've met our gross profit margin goal?
- Is our hand-off process from estimating to the field thorough enough? Does the hand-off process from estimating to the field provide sufficient information to allow foremen to successfully produce the job as budgeted, and as promised? Does it clearly communicate the estimated hours by cost code so the

foreman knows how many hours they have to complete the project?
- Are our contracts with customers and subcontractors set up to safeguard us as a company? Have we left loopholes or have we been unclear about what, precisely, they can expect from the deal?

SALES / MARKETING

- Do we have a written sales process (checklists are good) that gives the customer clarity regarding desired outcome, priorities, pricing, scope, and timing? Will it give the same for us?
- Have we clearly defined our sales and close rate percentage goals?
- Are we tracking results against those goals monthly? Download the "Bid and Close Rate Tracker" tool from my website https://the-profitbleed.com/resources at no charge.
- Do we know our backlog of signed work by month and are we tracking it against our operating budget (this is signed work that's either in process or scheduled for the future—there's a tab on the Bid Tracking Worksheet)? Am I tracking this backlog against my budgeted revenue projections (built into the Bid Tracking Worksheet)?

- Are we evaluating bid results every six months to a year to see if the people we're repeatedly preparing bids for are actually hiring us to do work or just using us to get a price?

PRODUCTION

- Do we have a tight change order process in place that ensures we don't do work that is not authorized by the customer with written agreements, i.e. signed field work authorizations and change orders?
- Are project two-week look-ahead reports completed every two weeks. If so, do they clearly spell out the next two-week critical milestones, actions, and plan? Download the "Two Week Look-Ahead Template" tool from my website https://theprofitbleed.com/resources at no charge.
- Do foremen and project managers sit down weekly with hours burned against budget reports and work out a plan for staying on budget?

FEEDBACK

- Does our company have an operating budget that accounts for the profits we want to be making?
- Is there an accounting calendar in place, and are deadlines managed such that project data is up to date by end of day each Friday?
- Do we get reporting on actual results compared to budget by the tenth of each month, and are we reading those reports? Do we manage the numbers for our company the way we would on a project to ensure we are meeting our profit goals?
- Do we review our balance sheet ratios each month to assess the financial health of our company? Get your free "cheat sheet" for what numbers to track on your profit and loss as well as balance sheet by visiting my website and downloading my article "How to Read Your Financial Reports:" at https://theprofitbleed.com/resources

PROJECT MANAGEMENT

- Are project schedules updated every two weeks with milestones and have labor and subcontractor resources been identified?

- Are project managers planning all client, team, and site visit meetings at least two weeks in advance? Do they have a specific date each month to review job reports?
- Do cost to complete projects get done by the end of the first week of each month, so you know where projects will end up on cost?

MAKE A PLAN

By now, you may have come up with a laundry list of things that need to be changed in your company. This insight, this laundry list of tasks, may feel a bit daunting, maybe even overwhelming. After all, this is often how my clients feel the first time we sit down and do the analysis together. They have no idea where to start.

"Believe it or not, you've done the hard work," I invariably tell them, just as I did with Constantine. "Most people don't even want to look at the truth. They'd rather stick their head in the sand than look at the numbers. You haven't done that. You've got a clear snapshot of reality so you can take action to change the outcome. It only gets easier from here." I explain. "Now it's time to break the proverbial elephant into bite-sized pieces. You cannot possibly take everything all at one time. You need to chunk it down into manageable bits."

How do you stop the profit bleed? What items do you choose from that laundry list first? You take on one project at a time to keep yourself sane. You make friends with the numbers.

THE SIMPLE TRUTH

You think that since you're working so hard the universe should reward your efforts, but that's not how business works. What makes business work is generating consistent profits, and having systems in place that create sustainability. And it's about clear communication. It's about knowing what feedback to look at so that you can keep your finger on the pulse and lifeblood of your company. It's focusing on the essentials. It's only when you do all these things that you get your just reward. It is *then* that you have the life you desire.

It's within your capability to accomplish this, and the first step is accepting that you don't need to kill yourself to get there. You don't need to put in more hours. That's just a harmful myth. You don't have to be the one to do the important stuff; you can actually delegate when you know how to do it right. More volume does not make for more profits; that's the thinking that's killing you. You need the right customers, the kind of jobs to which you're best suited.

Working all the time; fighting fires with a squirt gun; resenting the hell out of people who just aren't doing their jobs; undercutting your prices to win that lousy bid; hedging your bets; dealing with customers as though they're the enemy—it doesn't have to be this way.

If you're willing to embrace the concepts I've outlined for you here, you'll start to gain more control over the results in your business. You'll be in charge of your own destiny, no longer waiting for the universe to pay you your due reward. You'll be the master of your life. Learn to use your numbers to your benefit, as opposed to using them as a cudgel to beat yourself with. Have the discipline to manage by results—on a consistent basis.

When you do these things, you'll finally be clear and, as a result, more confident about what actions to take.

Let your competitors play the volume game, price themselves right out of business, continually hedge their bets, bleed right out onto the pavement. You know better now. You know which course corrections to take to get (and keep) you on the path to the success you want and deserve. After all, you've now got your finger on the pulse.

APPENDIX

Resources to help you stop the profit bleed in your company:

Available at: https://theprofitbleed.com/resources (unless otherwise indicated).

ESTIMATING

Knowing Your Real Costs of Running Your Business

Calculating Overhead Breakeven Percentage (PDF)— an easy to follow outline for how to calculate the real overhead breakeven percentage for your company, so you're clear on how much you must mark up bids just to break even.

How to Calculate Employee True Costs (Excel)—in addition to gross wages and taxes, there are many other costs that go into having an employee. Make sure you know your fully burdened cost for having that employee. Here is a link to one of Vicki's associate's website that has a calculator that can help you figure out this number: https://buildyournumbers.com/labor-burden-calculator-videos-ecpa-2ipa/

Mark up to Make a Profit

Mark up and Margin Explained (PDF)—this resource explains the difference between mark up and margin, and how to think about these differences when bidding and when analyzing project results.

Mark up and Margin Chart (PDF)—a simple chart referencing how much you need to mark up overall to reach your desired gross profit margin goal.

SALES

Sales Management Resources

The Sales Process (PDF)—an outline with suggested steps and questions to ask in each stage of the sales cycle from the time a call comes through contract signing. This template lets you gain control over the sales process, build trust with the prospect, and ultimately close more sales.

Bid, Close Rate and Backlog Tracker (Excel)—a tool for tracking bids completed, and won or lost, so you can easily see your pipeline as well as close rates. This template lets you easily set goals—and then manage results against those goals—with automated links. Review this report every two weeks.

PRODUCTION

Production Management Resources

Two-Week Look-Ahead Planner (Excel template)—helps you plan out the next two weeks in the field so foremen have a plan of what specific actions and results they need to accomplish in the next two weeks.

Production Reports to Review (PDF)—designed to help you keep your finger on the pulse of projects and stay in front of billings, costs, and client connection.

FINANCIAL MANAGEMENT

Financial Management Resources

How to Read Your Financial Reports (PDF)—a simple guide to understanding the story your numbers are telling when you look at an Income Statement (Profit & Loss) and Balance Sheet.

Budget to Cash Flow Template (Excel template)—a planning tool for setting specific and measurable goals for the coming year for income, gross profit margin, overhead expenses, and cash flow. This template includes detailed instruction that walk you through step-by-step in creating a plan for your increased profitability in the coming year. https://suiterbusinessbuilders.com/tools/templates/

Financial Reports to Review (PDF)—keep your finger on the pulse of your company's financial health by knowing which financial reports to review and when. This tells you not just the report, but what to look for on the report as well.

Sample Accounting Calendar (PDF)—plan out the month to stay in front of results.

KNOW WHERE YOU'RE BLEEDING PROFITS

Getting Your Finger on the Pulse

Business Health Assessment (Word and Excel Worksheets)—assessment tool that gives you the guidelines and questions to follow to assess the health of your company, to determine where your company is bleeding profits, and to help you identify what actions you can take to make it healthy.

■ ■ ■

DEFINITION OF KEY TERMS

Project Estimate/Budget—the calculated direct costs of producing a scope of work.

Markup—an amount added to the direct costs to determine the selling price.

Margin—the difference which exists between net sales and the cost of services sold and from which expenses are usually met or profit derived.

Overhead Breakeven Percentage—the percentage used to mark up direct costs to cover overhead expenses and *just* break even on the bottom line.

Hand-off Process—the communication of specifications, project details, assumptions, inclusions, exclusions, and client commitments from estimating/sales to production before a project begins.

Two-Week Look-Ahead—a process for looking at project milestones and critical path items to occur in the next two weeks, as well as a plan for ensuring those deadlines are met in the field.

Change Order—the client's written order, issued after execution of the construction contract, which authorizes a change in the construction work and contract time and/or amount.

Operating Budget—a combination of known expenses, expected future costs, and forecasted income over the course of a year.

Income Statement—accounting of the income and expenses that indicate a firm's net profit or loss over a certain period, usually one year.

Balance Sheet—a statement of the financial position of a business for a specified period that reflects the company's value or net worth from its inception.

Project Schedule—the tool that communicates what work needs to be performed, which resources of the organization will perform the work, and the timeframes in which that work needs to be performed. The project schedule should reflect all of the work associated with delivering the project on time.

Milestones—a marker in a project that signifies a change or stage in project development. Milestones are powerful components of a project plan because they show key events and map forward movement. They act as signposts throughout the course of your project to ensure you're staying on track.

Cost to Complete—the sum of the contract's cumulative to-date actual cost of work performed, plus project manager's best estimate of the funds required to complete the remaining authorized work.

Pulse Points—essential elements to monitor that will allow you to keep your finger on the pulse or health of your company.

ABOUT THE AUTHOR

International Speaker, Business Consultant and Coach, Vicki Suiter has been showing business owners and managers how to thrive, not just survive, for more than 25 years. Her motto? The key to success comes from gaining clarity in all areas of your business: appreciating where you are, deciding where you want to go, and making a plan to get there. Because when you commit to being clear, you've discovered the real secret to securing a successful future. With her ability to eliminate the extraneous, Vicki enables her clients to get a grip on their business vision from day one. And things just keep improving from there. It's all about understanding your numbers, establishing systems, and creating structures to support business growth.

In addition to building strong businesses, Vicki loves creating memorable meals. Her first book, *Mangia!...I Love You!* shares two generations of her family's well-guarded recipes. Creating a good business is just like cooking a delicious dish. You start with a clear idea and good ingredients. Then, even if it doesn't turn out exactly as you planned, you know everything will be OK. Her workshop "Cooking and Leadership" teaches business owners communication, planning, and leadership skills using cooking as the medium.

Vicki lives in Novato, California with her husband, Tim, and their dog, Nica. The mother of three awesome grown children, Vicki loves spending time with family when not empowering clients, writing, and speaking. Vicki can be contacted at: vicki@suiterbusinessbuilders.com.

CPSIA information can be obtained
at www.ICGtesting.com
Printed in the USA
FSHW02n1053171018
53083FS